TRIGGER⊢RESS

The voice of mental health

www.trigger-press.com

Thank you for purchasing this book.
You are making an incredible difference.

Proceeds from all Trigger Press books go directly to
The Shaw Mind Foundation, a global charity that focuses
entirely on mental health. To find out more about
The Shaw Mind Foundation visit **www.shawmindfoundation.org**

MISSION STATEMENT

Our goal is to make help and support available for every
single person in society, from all walks of life.
We will never stop offering hope. These are our promises.
Trigger Press and The Shaw Mind Foundation

the *Shaw* mind
FOUNDATION

Creating hope for children,
adults and families

Overcoming adversity and thriving

Today Just Like Yesterday
Defying Dysthymia One Challenge at a Time
BY RICHARD KIRBY

We are proud to introduce The**inspirational**series™. Part of the Trigger Press family of innovative mental health books, The**inspirational**series™ tells the stories of the people who have battled and beaten mental health issues. For more information visit: www.trigger-press.com

THE AUTHOR

Richard Kirby was born in York in 1964 and lives near Middlesbrough, UK. He was diagnosed with depression in 2004; however, a decade later he found out that his condition was actually dysthymia, a mild but chronic form of depression.

Having first revealed his mental health issues in 2011, Richard began to both write and talk openly about his feelings and how the condition affected his life. Then, in 2014, he embarked on a series of "challenges" designed to raise mental health awareness. Four years and 100 challenges later, Richard now has the chance to tell his story and prove that it is possible to find the strength to fight back ...

First published in Great Britain 2018 by Trigger Press

Trigger Press is a trading style of Shaw Callaghan Ltd & Shaw Callaghan 23 USA, INC.

The Foundation Centre

Navigation House, 48 Millgate, Newark

Nottinghamshire NG24 4TS UK

www.trigger-press.com

British Library Cataloguing in Publication Data

A CIP catalogue record for this book is available upon request
from the British Library

ISBN: 978-1-911246-61-9

This book is also available in the following e-Book formats:

MOBI: 978-1-911246-64-0

EPUB: 978-1-911246-62-6

PDF: 978-1-911246-63-3

Song lyrics from 'The Close' reproduced with the kind permission from The Alarm

Cover design and typeset by Fusion Graphic Design Ltd

Project Management by Out of House Publishing

Printed and bound in Great Britain by Bell & Bain, Glasgow

Paper from responsible sources

Today, just like yesterday
I'm ascending and descending
Travelling, not arriving
That's the story of my life ...

For Mum, Dad and Elaine xxx

FOREWORD

One in four people in the UK have mental health problems. Nearly two thirds of these never seek help from a medical professional.

As a sufferer of a form of chronic depression himself, Richard has worked tirelessly to bring about positive changes in the perception and treatment of mental ill health. His fundraising for the charity Mind in 2014 – and his dedication to the Time to Change campaign – have both made a significant impact on the stigma attached to mental health issues.

When Richard approached me to fulfil his "Meet an Olympic Gold Medallist" challenge, I was delighted to have the opportunity to meet this extraordinary man – who is, himself, a source of inspiration, especially because of the positive and proactive way he has reached out to other sufferers and spoken openly about his mental health.

His dreams of taking on 100 challenges to highlight mental health were close to my heart, as my parents were psychiatric nurses in a hospital near our home (before moves were made to set up Care in the Community). I spent many happy times as a child / teenager in the company of patients, many of whom never had visitors – such was the stigma attached to their illness.

This book is a triumphant record of his outstanding contribution to mental health awareness, and I am proud to be a very small part of it.

Ann Brightwell (née Packer) MBE
800m gold medallist and 400m silver medallist at the 1964 Tokyo Olympic Games.
July 2017

INTRODUCTION

I was diagnosed with depression in 2004. It was a label I hated.

It's not that I hated *officially* having a mental health condition. I just felt deeply guilty because, in my own mind, I wasn't "ill" enough for my doctor to tell me I was clinically depressed. I had evidently been unwell for a while, but I associated the word depression with far worse symptoms than those I was suffering from at that time.

That original diagnosis of depression came during a particularly difficult time in my life. Those closest to me could see there was something wrong, but I wouldn't listen – I'd never needed help before, so I insisted that I didn't need it then ...

But I *did* need help.

Looking back, the downward spiral took hold so quickly, but somehow (and I honestly don't know how), I had one brief moment of objective clarity, and with it came the realisation that I could no longer cope. I made an appointment to see my doctor and literally, within seconds of sitting down in front of him, I broke down completely.

I was given a handful of counselling sessions, but for whatever reason they did nothing but leave me feeling drained and heavy-headed. I eventually decided to stop. It was right for me to at least give this method of treatment a shot, but it was equally as sensible to give it up when it was obviously having a negative effect on me.

My medication *did* work though. Over time, my depression disappeared. And it was then that I realised the importance of that initial visit to the surgery. Because just over a decade later – after a lot of research, therapy, GP visits and lengthy discussions with experts in mental health – I realised I had dysthymia. I had always had it.

My depression was just the upper layer of what is called "double depression". When that – the "upper layer" – was effectively treated, my dysthymia (the "lower layer") remained unconsidered, undetected, hidden. Waiting for an opportunity to resurface.

Dysthymia is a chronic, but relatively mild, form of depression from which I had almost certainly – and unknowingly – suffered since junior school. The characteristics of dysthymia are not dissimilar to depression, although they are less intense and extreme. I'd had symptoms for 40 years or so, and because I essentially knew no different, I'd always presumed that how I felt was "normal".

Since as far back as my teenage years, I have suffered from anxiety and panic attacks. I've also experienced occasional bouts of sudden and profound sadness. I liken the sensation to a giant hand gripping my head, squeezing ever tighter and forcing me to cry.

As this happened more and more, I began to accept my tears rather than fight them. I got to a point where I not only wanted to cry, I *needed* to. Often, I would hide away and let the tears flow until the hand eventually relaxed its grip.

Over the years this continued to happen – throughout my childhood, during my married life and through the birth of my two wonderful daughters.

So much has changed since 2004, and mostly for the better. I no longer have depression – which is great, despite my lingering dysthymia – and I'm now married to the love of my life.

I met Elaine at a work training day in December 2004. We stayed in touch, but didn't see each other again until the following October. People will have their own idea about "love at first sight", but from that chilly October evening in 2005 to the day I moved down from

Gateshead to Middlesbrough to begin a new life with her in July 2006, we saw each other fewer than 10 times.

We married in 2008, and Elaine has made the most amazing difference to my life.

As a random aside, the register office in Guisborough – where our wedding ceremony took place – is now part of a national pub chain. (I did say it was random …)

As Big Ben's 12th bong heralded the arrival of 2014, I was all too aware that just a few months later I would reach my 50th birthday. I didn't particularly relish the prospect, but nonetheless it was a milestone I wanted to commemorate in some way ("celebrate" doesn't quite feel like the right word!).

Courtesy of a rare flash of inspiration, the idea of setting myself a series of "challenges" started to develop in the last few weeks of 2013, and by the start of the new year it had grown into a list of at least 40 tasks.

I've often been asked how I came up with the concept of setting myself a variety of challenges, tasks and new experiences. It's a request I've honestly done everything I can to ignore, but sometimes you simply have to shrug your shoulders and say, 'Well, you did ask …'

I was lying in the bath.

Strictly speaking I was *having* a bath … in water. I hadn't just clambered into an empty bath in the hope it would give me some sudden inspiration.

Probably best to move on now …

The truth is that it was simply a random idea that popped into my head without warning. But once the seed had been sown, I quickly became excited and started thinking about all the possible challenges I could take on.

I wondered about how I could give the project some sort of mental health focus. At this point I was still a few months away from discovering that I had dysthymia, but my history of depression and chronic low mood motivated me to raise mental health awareness by sharing my achievements online, in the media and with friends. And so I got in touch with Mind, the mental health charity. I offered to campaign and fundraise on their behalf, and they gave me the go-ahead.

This was it. I knew there was no turning back.

I also wanted to include some physical challenges among a pretty wide variety of tasks, all of which I designed to push myself. My sporting days (such as they were) had been brought to an abrupt end a few years before. I'd had aches and pains for a long time and eventually I got diagnosed with femoroacetabular impingement – a degenerative hip condition that will inevitably result in one or more joint replacements. Despite this though, I was in fairly good health and I wanted to give my ageing body one last push. I'm a huge sports fan, so it seemed only fitting.

I wanted each challenge to give me either a brand-new experience or, alternatively, some kind of a test – whether it was mental, emotional, physical or something that required a great deal of planning. The common theme (which reinforced the mental health focus) was that to fulfil most of the challenges, I would need to ask for help – maybe from someone I didn't know very well (or at all) – just as I had in that doctor's surgery almost a decade earlier.

The link between having a bird of prey fly onto my hand (by way of one example) and mental health may seem tenuous to some but – for me at least – mental health underpinned the whole project. That's what kept me going. There also seemed to be a close parallel between struggles associated with various types of mental illness and overcoming seemingly insurmountable obstacles to accomplish something beyond my own realistic expectations.

That said, right from the outset I knew there would be a few occasions when I would have to face my lifelong fear of failure.

The prospect of two tasks in particular filled me with dread. But the fact that I decided to undertake those first 40 tasks on behalf of Mind gave me a strong sense of purpose and a real determination to succeed.

Maybe I couldn't guarantee success. Maybe there were different levels of success, but the one thing I knew for certain was that I would achieve nothing if I didn't try ...

By 2017, my initial list of challenges had grown to 100 (full details are given at the end of the book), and as well as being involved with Mind during 2014, I was subsequently able to work closely with the Time to Change programme, which does such a fantastic job in challenging stigma and transforming how people think and talk about mental health.

The aim of this book is not only to offer an insight into what it is like to have dysthymia, but also to look back at the past four years and the stories behind some of the challenges. I want to show you how one idea, at the back end of 2013, ended up actually changing my life.

My hope is that the concept makes you stop and think from time to time, while providing a chuckle or two along the way. More importantly, I want to demonstrate that however daunting the prospect, it is fine to not only talk about mental health, but also to reach out and ask for help. Dysthymia will never go away ... but it doesn't have to stop you finding the strength to fight back.

CHAPTER 1

GROWING PAINS

It's only with the benefit of hindsight that I realise just how long I've had a mental health condition.

I've got a lot of random and sometimes unpleasant memories from when I was a kid – from as early as when I was 10 or 11 years old – and I now realise that they're the earliest signs of dysthymia.

Sometimes, in school, I would have moments where I'd feel hot and clammy. I'd get lightheaded and increasingly panicky, thinking I was going to pass out (thankfully I never did). It would happen when we were going into the school chapel or lining up in a queue. It made me really anxious because I couldn't just turn and walk away from the situation. At the time I just assumed it was a normal part of growing up, and I don't think I ever spoke about it.

I suppose mood swings and personality changes were inevitable when I was a teenager, but I think the nature of my upbringing inadvertently played a part in the issues I developed. My father was a teacher at my private school, and for some of that time he was also a boarding housemaster. Essentially this meant that home and school were one and the same place for me (there were no fees for sons of staff in the 1970s!). Every afternoon the day pupils would return to the relative sanctuary of their respective homes, while the boarders, at least, had plenty of company as a substitute for living apart from their parents. And even if they found it difficult, the next holiday break was never too far away.

But it was different for me. I could never leave. And being a teacher's son didn't make me overly popular …

Dad was strict but always fair. Unfortunately, the latter fact was of no consequence to some of my contemporaries, and I was on the receiving end of an awful lot of hurtful comments – and a punch or two along the way. I don't want to overstate the physical side of things. It happened, but not often, and it was no big deal physically – the pain never lasted very long – but the mental scars from all the insults were much harder to shrug off.

Much as I tried to avoid those who saw me as "fair game", I can recall the sickly feeling in the pit of my stomach when I realised that the person or people coming towards me were likely to stop and "exchange pleasantries". I will freely admit that their sneering insults bothered me. And while these incidents were probably nothing too significant in isolation, the fact that the same thing happened over and over again began to take its toll. As a result, I can still remember the names of those who will have long since forgotten I ever existed. At the time, I probably resented my parents for putting me in such a situation, but the truth is that they were doing what they've always done – the best they possibly could.

I started to become quite withdrawn, and by the time I turned 14 I was beginning to suffer periods of inexplicable sadness, the likes of which I still get to this day. My release was (and always has been) to cry.

I always knew when the tears were coming, and I gradually learnt just to let them flow rather than fighting them. Because however hard I fought, I could never hold them back.

But once the proverbial floodgates had opened, I'd fight just as hard to make sure I cried for as long as possible. I would force negative thoughts to the front of my mind, or I would play certain songs that struck an emotional chord.

A part of me, out of desperation, almost *wanted* to be found in a bad state. But I was so good at hiding how I felt that (to the best of my knowledge) no one ever knew ...

This is a difficult paradox that even now I can't readily explain.

Four decades later, I know that I have a mental health condition. I know its name and I know how it can affect me. All that is far removed from how things were in my teens, so in a sense I suppose it's reasonable to suggest I am very much a different person now.

That said, the more I reflect on those times, the prouder I become of the boy – the young man – who did his best to cope with occasionally extreme emotions that he couldn't fully understand. Maybe he was even brave? And if so, perhaps that's where the paradox lies. Because, while that person was undeniably me, it's hard to relate to the teenager who seems to have possessed a quality that I don't see in my adult self.

There was just one time when the taunting and mocking got too much. Memories of what was actually said are vague. Perhaps it was a case of one insult too many, but whatever the case, I just went into a complete state of panic. I hurried home, scribbled a note saying I was leaving to stay with my gran (with whom I always had a really close relationship) in Darlington, and set off for the train station. Everything was such a blur, I have no idea whether I even had the money for a ticket.

When I got to the station, I spotted Dad and my housemaster. They were clearly looking for me, but my head was in such a mess that my immediate thought was, *how did they know where to find me*? (Even though I'd left a note!)

It seems ridiculous, but I was totally lost and the only thing I wanted to do was run.

So I did ... all the way to a friend's house another mile or so away, where I finally crumbled.

I have no recollection of what happened after that. I can't remember what my parents said to me, or what I said to them, but it was probably the first time I'd done something that had really worried and upset them.

Perhaps my recent and gradual revelation of my inner has given my parents some belated insight into the child I was and the adult I have become.

In truth, by the time I was originally diagnosed, they probably had an idea that I had some sort of mental health condition, but although they were always completely supportive, the subject was rarely discussed in any great detail until the start of my challenges.

Since then though, we have chatted at length about the symptoms and effects of dysthymia. Both Mum and Dad were born before the outbreak of the Second World War, and therefore grew up in an era when there was little understanding of mental health and even less conversation. But even though it must have been difficult to listen to my troubles at times – it must have been upsetting to hear their son talk so openly – they simply listened and told me how proud they were. Even in my fifties, it was still lovely to get parental approval.

We are now closer than ever, and I'm so fortunate to be able to call them Mum and Dad. They are two very special people who I love with all my heart.

CHAPTER 2

PROZAC AND SPEED

For probably the majority of people who live with a mental health condition (myself included), life presents a daily challenge that can't simply be ticked off a list. Mental illness is something you must deal with every single day. Eventually it gets to a point where you can't hide it any more, and the best thing to do is be open and honest with other people. In December 2011 I had reached this point, and I wrote the following blog post – essentially my "big reveal" about my mental health issues.

So much that has happened since can be traced back to these words.

At the end of a week when the world of football (and beyond) has been paying tribute to Gary Speed, I would like to share a personal moment from these past seven days.

Recently, I've been suffering from several bouts of unexplained sadness. It's difficult to describe, but I would liken it to my head being squeezed until only negative emotions are left. I took a trip to the doctor who increased my antidepressant dosage in the hope (expectation, even) that my mood would stabilise.

In fact, the opposite happened. The good days were brilliant, but when the low came, it was horrible.

At 3.00am the following Thursday morning, I found myself alone in a Birmingham hotel room (for a work course), sobbing uncontrollably down the phone to Elaine. I wanted nothing but to catch the next train home from New Street to be with her. I couldn't explain why the tears wouldn't stop, let alone why they had started in the first place. The descent was fast enough to be frightening, in hindsight.

And when a feeling like that passes, the worst thing is the knowledge of the upset you have caused.

I am lucky that I have real (and metaphorical) shoulders to lean on. I also accept that, at the moment, I need medical support to get better. Believe me, taking antidepressants is not something I'm proud of, but I'm not ashamed either. Acceptance is the first and biggest step on the road to recovery – and recover is what I intend to do, even though I realise there will be difficult days along the way ...

I went back to the doctor's surgery last Friday and it resulted in a chat with a different GP, one who was prepared to take the time to listen and not judge – and wasn't willing to simply type out a prescription and shout, 'Next!'

The outcome? We realised that the double dose of Prozac was almost certainly responsible for my emotional extremes. No wonder I felt so inconsolable on Wednesday.

Knowing that the medication was partly to blame is a relief in itself, but it doesn't stop me from feeling guilty that others were affected by the state I was in.

Since then, my dosage has been halved again and I've been given some helpful lifestyle advice, so I see no reason why I shouldn't emerge from this difficult period very soon and get back to being my normal, grumpy, miserable self!

I have absolutely no idea what demons drove Gary Speed to take his own life. Was his suicide a coward's way out? Some will say so, but I don't agree. I have a small understanding of the power of the mind. Many never experience those kinds of dark thoughts. Others can fight them off, but a few find them almost impossible to ignore. Gary Speed's circumstances are none of my business, but I salute him as a proud and brave man – in life and in death. I sincerely hope that his family and closest friends find a way of dealing with the unimaginable sadness of the whole situation.

So, I dedicate this blog to the memory of the late Gary Speed, and to those whose love and support mean so much to me.

Writing this blog post felt really intense. Recalling how I had felt – and then finding the right words to convey those emotions – certainly didn't come naturally or easily. But sharing my experiences definitely gave me some perspective, as did telling the terrible story of a life lost in such awful circumstances. It strengthened my resolve and I was able to finish and post the article.

As far as any potential reactions to my blog post were concerned, I don't remember giving it a great deal of thought. I *knew* that virtually all my friends and most of my family were about to get a glimpse of the "real" me, but perhaps I (naively) expected that Gary's loss would overshadow or mask my own revelations. I certainly didn't want to *compare* my own situation to Gary's.

It didn't take too long for the first comments to appear – some were posted publicly, but a number were also sent privately. They were so supportive and I was amazed and genuinely moved by the response. It was enough for me that people had even read the blog – but the fact that they'd then taken the time to write a message to me afterwards helped to convince me that I'd made the right decision in being so open about my condition.

What was lovely was that the responses came from so many different parts of my life. I heard from people in my family and friends I'd met through playing cricket, watching rugby league and going to gigs. It was such a diverse mix of people, all brought together by the subject of mental health.

One of the first messages came from Paul "Bez" Berryman, who had been both my teammate and opponent during our respective cricket careers:

Well written, and I had no idea you suffered from depression. You take care and stay strong. Just remember that you bowled the best ball I have ever faced, and I've been playing for 32 years now.

(Bez has now been playing for 38 years, and to the best of my knowledge, he hasn't yet been dismissed by a better delivery. It's nice to know that someone remembers one of my good days, because I didn't half bowl some rubbish over the years!)

This next post was one of the most emotive:

Wow! Such a powerful post, Richard! [You've] got me in tears here. I am very proud of the frank and open way that you talk about your illness. Depression is a wicked thing and something I suffer from myself. I know that when you get the unbearable lows it's the people and friends in your life that give you the strength to get through the next second, minute, hour. It's a difficult thing for anyone who has not experienced this to understand ...

Given the personal nature of the message, it wouldn't be right to reveal the name of the person who posted this. The same also applies to this final comment ... mainly because it was posted by Anonymous!

Well written. I do know you – and can understand some of what you have written – but I could not have said these words any better. You should be proud of yourself for having the courage to share your feelings with others and hopefully help others who may be suffering in the same way.

I came back to these comments when writing this book, and realised that I hadn't read them (and all the others) in nearly six years. But their kind and positive words still resonate today.

And so, however tough it was to write the original blog post, there is no doubt that some of my inspiration, strength and belief in myself

– all of which eventually led me to devote so much time to raising mental health awareness – can be attributed to those people who left me messages back in 2011. In hindsight, it really was a major turning point ...

CHAPTER 3

STARTING THE CHALLENGES

RAISE £1,000 FOR MIND CHARITY

By definition, my efforts to raise £1,000 for Mind began at the start of January 2014 and, as the target wasn't achieved until early November, it must be the task that took the longest to successfully complete. Obviously, I had been in contact with Mind before any of the challenges were attempted, as it was important that the charity was happy with what I was intending to do to raise money on their behalf. In truth, they were very supportive and got in touch at various points throughout the year to see how things were going, and to ask if I needed any help ... or a t-shirt.

I never turn down a t-shirt.

Some people are natural fundraisers; sadly, I'm not one of them. I couldn't expect mental health and Mind to have the same relevance and resonance for all my family and friends as it did for me. And in addition, there were (and still are) so many people doing amazing things to raise money for any number of worthwhile causes that over the months that followed, I regularly questioned whether the bar had been set too high.

I was also going to have to demonstrate that I was serious about completing all 40 challenges. I couldn't just get a tweet from a Spice

Girl (the first challenge I did), sit back and expect the cash to start rolling in.

Donations tended to be received only after certain tasks had been accomplished – maybe they were considered the most interesting or testing. On a handful of occasions, a sizeable sum was pledged, which I must admit made me feel incredibly humble. I got steadily closer to my target until, in the first week in November 2014, one significant contribution took the total to within a few pounds of the magic number. One more donation later and I broke the £1,000 barrier.

The final amount raised for Mind was £1,064.04.

I've wracked my brains, but I've absolutely no idea where the extra 4p came from!

RECEIVE A TWEET FROM A SPICE GIRL

And here it is: my very first task to be ticked off my list back in January 2014.

I was on Twitter at the time (fairly obviously), but very much a novice. I can't really remember why I decided to base a challenge around the Spice Girls, but at least the odds of receiving a reply were better than if I'd chosen a solo artist. As you will have gathered, I'm partial to a ramble, and limiting messages to 140 characters was actually a challenge in itself.

But without holding out too much hope, I sat down in front of my laptop and typed out four individual messages explaining what I was hoping to achieve over the next 12 months (actually, I ended up attaching a link to the explanation. I'd barely finished saying "hello" and nearly half of my allotted characters had gone).

Just four minutes after the last message had been sent, I received a reply … from Melanie Chisholm (aka Mel C or Sporty Spice), which read:

Melanie C ⊙
@MelanieCmusic

[+ Follow] ⌄

Hey @kirbs1964 Good luck with your mission Rich! #SpiceUpYourLife! x

1:42 AM - 4 Jan 2014

4 Retweets **18** Likes

♡ 4   ⇄ 4   ♡ 18   ✉

The project was officially underway. And I have to say I was really #chuffed ...

CHAPTER 4

FINGER ON THE PULSE

APPEAR ON A RADIO SHOW

In January 2014 I emailed BBC Radio Tees to see if they might be interested in my story. They didn't only say yes, but they also invited me on to a live show!

Writing about personal experiences isn't particularly easy, but it is something you can get used to with practice. Talking about them (essentially to strangers) is another thing altogether. It's hard and it's scary.

But I knew that if I was going to do all my challenges justice (both individually and collectively), then it was important to face, head-on, those things that I'd probably prefer to avoid. I guess that's the very essence of what makes some of my tasks "challenges".

I was to appear on Mike Parr's morning programme and, when I arrived, I was shown to the studio by one of the producers. I had made a few crib notes beforehand, in case the words dried up when I was faced with a microphone. I was far more nervous than I'd expected.

I even checked my pulse, because it felt unusually fast.

It *was* unusually fast.

Mike did his best to make me feel more at ease, but when the music stopped and he introduced me, there was a moment's panic as to whether I'd actually be able to speak. Thankfully, the words did come, and we discussed some of my challenges before moving on to the more serious part of the conversation.

I must admit that talking so openly about the symptoms and effects of my condition wasn't as difficult as I'd imagined – perhaps that was because I was focusing on the one person I could see, rather than imagining how many might be listening.

I was still acutely aware that I was freely revealing personal details that I'd fought so hard and so long to hide. But I accepted that if my efforts at raising awareness were to gain any level of credibility, I would, on occasion, have to completely remove my mask. I had to prove to the listeners that it was okay.

Our chat was interrupted briefly by some travel news (I think – it totally passed me by). It was all over really quickly. Both Mike and the producer (who was listening in the adjoining studio) told me that my nervousness didn't come across during the interview – which was a major relief.

When I got home that evening, I listened to the interview and was pleasantly surprised at how I sounded. On the few previous occasions when I'd heard my recorded voice, it had seemed gruff and rather dull, but the BBC Tees Radio microphone somehow gave me a softer tone that really helped to convey the message. I posted a link to the programme on social media and received a number of positive comments from family and friends about the content of the interview. But sadly no one mentioned my film-star voice!

PRESENT A RADIO SHOW

It seemed, to me, that the logical progression from appearing on a radio show was to be involved in some aspect of presenting a programme.

27

I was grateful to be put in touch with Gareth Cooper, who was one of the driving forces behind a monthly show called *Mentally Sound*. It was, at the time, broadcast from the studios of Gravity Radio North East in Newcastle city centre. We spoke on the phone and, to my delight, Gareth invited me to co-host the next edition of the show – an opportunity that was far too good to miss, especially given the programme's mental health theme.

Mentally Sound was being transmitted on the second Friday of every month, and was still in its relative infancy – the next instalment would be show number six. Behind the scenes there was a small but dedicated team, determined to try to raise the profile of hugely important (and often personal) issues through a combination of live guests, topical discussion and pre-recorded inserts. These were punctuated with slightly less relevant – but nonetheless enjoyable – tunes along the way.

Gareth and producer Victoria McGowan completed the pre-show preparations and I sat down in what was a decidedly warm studio, opposite the presenter Steven Heslewood, Steven was supposed to brief me as to my involvement in the proceedings, but we'd mostly nattered about wrestling instead. Last, but absolutely not least, I met Wayne Madden – the master of all things technical. Which was just as well, because as the show started my microphone wasn't working!

In fairness, it could always have been a pre-arranged plan: 'Don't switch it on until you're sure he's not going to be crap!'

Thankfully, Wayne got the thing fixed and soon all was well. Steven introduced me to the listeners and I gave a bit of background about my dysthymia and why I wanted to take on the various challenges. I had so much that I wanted to say, but the next eight minutes seemed to fly by. All too soon it was time for the first of the pre-recorded interviews.

Ricky Kumar then came into the studio to give a topical news update. This was then used to prompt discussions between the three of us – with seamless links from Steven allowing the second microphone to be redirected between me and Ricky. The theory was that this would prevent any unnatural break in conversation. Who knew radio could be so complicated?

There was one particularly interesting part of the show, namely when a second live guest came in to talk about his love of writing – specifically his undeniably intriguing dual-themed book about King Arthur's legend and mental health, all apparently set in a modern nightclub.

You might just want to read that last paragraph again!

Interestingly, some of the best conversation probably happened off-air. Steven, Ricky, Wayne and I all continued to debate some of the points that had been raised while the audience listened to the pre-recorded material. Perhaps strict adherence to a schedule gave the presenters some assurance, especially from having most of the content ready at the press of a button. But I did feel that more live interaction might have interested the readers more, especially if it offered an opportunity to delve deeper into the various mental-health-related topics that had featured in the actual broadcast.

The following year, I had the chance to see how far the show had developed first-hand when I joined Steven for a second stint behind the microphone.

Instalment number 12 included a few songs and a two-minute recorded introduction to Lexie Thorpe's fascinating piece on *anorexia nervosa*. Lexie began by defining the term "anorexia" (in its basic form, a loss of appetite that can often be treated by addressing an underlying medical condition), before explaining the differences in symptoms and treatment when the word "nervosa" is added. I ignorantly believed the two conditions were one and the same, but it is *anorexia nervosa* that is the avoidance of eating caused by a fear of gaining weight or poor body image. It's this condition that will usually cause the sufferer to require some form of psychiatric treatment.

The remainder of the show was built around live conversation with the guests (and a bit of what I believe is called "banter" between host and co-host). The guests were brilliant. As well as Lexie there was Colin Dolan, who'd travelled over from Liverpool to talk about his work based around football therapy for people experiencing mental health problems. Colin's own life experiences with depression, as well as the remarkable work he was doing, made for genuinely compelling listening.

In fairness, you could have built a two-hour show entirely around the links between mental health (or mental strength) and sport, but as the show progressed, it became clear that the same could also be said about some of the other subjects that were covered.

Those topics comprised intriguing research into the possible causes of schizophrenia, some superb work being undertaken to support local carers, and information about dementia. Ricky popped in for his regular news update and picked what I thought were particularly interesting stories, and finally there was information about some sort of role-playing game that thankfully resonated with Steven ... because I didn't understand it at all!

For a time, it felt like the guests were coming in and out on a conveyor belt – thankfully Victoria had everything under control. But even though all the live content was a bit of an added pressure for Steven, he made everyone feel comfortable. And the obvious interest he had in the various subjects afforded a natural flow to the conversations, which I hope came across to those listening. (Certainly, the show's Twitter feed was getting positive comments during transmission.) It really was a very good show and it made me realise just how many different people are touched by the subject of mental health.

I'd been nervous enough just talking into a radio microphone, but how would I have felt if I'd been in a live television studio environment? I did wonder what it might be like to look into a camera knowing that literally everything you said – every single facial expression –

was being beamed into countless homes across the region or maybe even the entire country.

Well, two and a half years later, I found out ...

APPEAR ON TELEVISION

Looking at this challenge simplistically, it seemed logical (at least to me) that the task would be reasonably easy to accomplish, seeing as it only contained three words. But as the weeks and then months passed, it began to look like I would have to stand behind a news reporter during a live outside broadcast, doing a silly wave or some sort of comedy walk to put the tick in the number 88 box.

However, at Elaine's request, I made an application to a quiz show in late 2016. That eventually led to me completing the challenge nearly nine long months later.

The show in question was *The Chase*, and that initial application led to an audition in York in March 2017. I managed to get through that stage of the process, but this was still no guarantee of actually being selected to appear on the show. Apparently, though, as tens of thousands of people had applied, that meant that we were "already winners".

I heard nothing for several months. In fact, I'd pretty much forgotten about the programme, but in July 2017 – totally out of the blue – I received a call from one of the researchers asking for additional background information. We had some more conversations over the subsequent weeks, until finally I was offered a place on an upcoming recording.

I was thrilled to be given an offer, despite the fact that it prompted yet more calls to finalise travel and accommodation arrangements. We'd be making the trip to Elstree Studios in Borehamwood during September.

For those who have never seen the show, the format goes a bit like this: there is a team of four who each answer a bunch of general knowledge questions before facing a quiz expert (the Chaser). The number of questions you get right in this first round eventually determines how many spaces ahead of the Chaser you are in a game of cat and mouse, which involves a round of much harder multiple-choice questions. The Chaser will try to entice you into staying closer to him or her by offering you more money, essentially making the prize for beating them even better. He or she will also offer you less money for moving further away from them. In order to take the money into the final round, you have to run – and stay away – from them by getting your questions right. If you get one wrong and he or she gets it right, they will move closer to you. The idea is to "get back home" to join your teammates, bringing a decent sum of money along with you. If the Chaser catches you, that's it; you leave the game.

Those of you in your team who have managed to outrun your adversaries go to the "final chase" – two more minutes of quick-fire questions. The Chaser then has two minutes to beat your score. If he or she does, you win nothing. But if they fail to catch you, however much money you have accumulated is split evenly between the number of winning contestants.

The good news was that Elaine could come down and stay at the hotel, but sadly she wouldn't be allowed inside the studio. We duly drove down to Hertfordshire on the day before the recording (we had to stay overnight because we'd be getting picked up for the studio at seven o'clock in the morning!).

I didn't sleep very well. There was loads of quiz-related stuff whizzing round and round in my head and it completely disturbed my rest. I got up early and made it to the foyer. James, one of the staff members from the show, was already there, as was Jessica, one of my team members from Norwich. The other two contestants (Liz from Uxbridge and Ash from Stockport) arrived soon afterwards. They all seemed nice enough people, and I had the chance to have a bit of chat with them all throughout the day. It helped to have such a friendly team with me, as I was starting to feel nervous.

As an aside, the first person we saw as the taxi pulled up outside the studio door was Jake Wood (Max Branning in *EastEnders*). I also spotted Linda Henry (Shirley Carter) after having my make-up applied. I'm glad I looked my best for her ...

Sam, Annie and James were entrusted with looking after us. They were with us for the whole six hours, and were positive and supportive throughout. We had to bring five different outfits, all of which were camera-tested (to make sure the colours would work on television, and patterns would not strobe), before one was chosen for us. Mine was an orange linen shirt. 10 pounds well spent ...

I never knew there was this level of preparation for a TV show.

We were given plenty of advice about the kind of things we should or shouldn't say and the type of interaction Bradley Walsh wanted, to ensure the edited show was as entertaining as possible. We were told our podium position (I was to be the second contestant), and then it was off to make-up. Funnily enough, it didn't take long to dab my face with some powder, mainly because half my face was hidden by the stubble I hadn't removed because I'd forgotten to pack my shaver.

Any call of nature required a series of intercom conversations to make sure the coast was clear (i.e. there were no Chasers on the loose), but as soon as you reached the studio, toilet breaks were not permitted.

And that's why I skipped breakfast ...

Seeing the set for the first time was a surreal moment (the first of many). It was smaller than it appears on the television screen, and you are quite a bit closer to the Chaser than you might suspect from watching the programme. We had a brief walk round the set and met the independent adjudicator and floor manager, before having our microphones attached. It all started feeling rather real as we took our seats at the desk (if that's the right word), behind our brightly illuminated names.

Our first job was to do a short introduction to one of the number of cameras positioned around the set. Three of the team did theirs perfectly; I think you can guess the odd one out!

Sam, Annie and James then reappeared – as they would at every break in proceedings – with water and welcome words of encouragement. There was also a warning not to spill any water on our clothing, as that would result in filming having to be halted while the offending top was dried. Thankfully no one dribbled.

Bradley Walsh came over to introduce himself and give us a bit of a pep talk. We'd been told that he was as nice in real life as he appeared on the screen, and just a short time in his company seemed to confirm that for me.

Brad (as he liked to be called) read his introduction from the autocue, returned to his seat to the side of the Chaser's set, and then reappeared a couple of minutes later to record the first contestant's "cash builder" round. Liz was in seat number one. She had a chat with Brad that lasted maybe two or three minutes, but would later be edited down to a minute or so, before it was time for her quick-fire questions.

I lost count of the number of times before, during and after the day that we were told not to disclose the result of the show in a public forum. I'm guessing a book counts as reasonably public, so at the risk of disappointing, upsetting or even annoying readers, I will comply with those requests … well, most of them.

We were led to believe that the host and most of the crew had no idea which Chaser we would be facing, and as three shows are filmed in a day, there would be more than one Chaser in the studio at any one time. The advice we were given was to show some reaction when the Chaser emerged for the first time – advice I ignored completely as Paul Sinha (aka The Sinnerman) appeared and walked forward to take his seat overlooking Liz.

He was actually quite complimentary to all four contestants during the recording. There was no mock-confrontational banter and thankfully no one said, 'bring it on', or any other similar phrase. I had made my mind up to be as humble as possible throughout the process; I certainly wasn't going to try to come up with a smart comment, the likes of which are so often followed by a string of wrong answers and an embarrassing exit stage right.

After Liz had faced Paul, it was my turn …

Cue water, make-up, some final words of advice … and some gel for a stray grey hair that seemingly glistened on camera.

We had to stand with our feet either side of a couple of strips of tape on the floor. I was really nervous, but got through my chat with Brad, during which I was able to mention that I'd spent a lot of my spare time raising mental health awareness by undertaking a series of tasks and challenges. I explained that I'd done some stand-up comedy and sparred with a professional boxer, but that the latter had got more laughs. It was slightly contrived, but a nice way to make sure that mental health was part of the conversation!

It was a major relief when the cash builder round got underway and I answered my first question correctly. Somehow that made the rest of it more manageable. It's weird, but I can't remember all the questions I was asked, although there was one about a member of McFly who'd written a children's book. I gave the correct answer – Tom Fletcher – and got an approving nod from the host. I passed on a question when I could have guessed the right answer, but I was more than happy with seven correct responses in 60 seconds.

It was then time for another break before facing The Sinnerman. The buttons used for the next section of the programme are much smaller than you might imagine. They were like a computer keyboard – presumably so neither party can try to work out what answer the other has pressed. The letters A, B and C were written in biro on little bits of paper stuck to the buttons – all very hi-tech – but it was obviously important to watch what you were doing when the time came to select an answer.

Cue dramatic music and Paul's reappearance. He seemed impressed by the Tom Fletcher answer, and gave me a higher offer of £35,000 to stay nearer to him during the chase (not that the bare numbers felt like actual cash at any stage). I can't remember the lower offer, but this was the point when I had to ask the rest of the team which offer I should accept. To do this, I had to turn 180 degrees to my right to face them (sounds easy, but we actually had to practise beforehand!) and then a left-hand turn back. Again, I'm not sure what was said, but there was no way I was ever going to take a lower offer, and £7,000 was too much to gamble.

The chase was on ...

The first question was easy, but my hand was shaking and I nearly pressed the wrong button! From then on though, I wasn't certain of any of the answers, and my responses ranged from educated to total stab-in-the-dark guesses.

After each question you are supposed to give a really interesting explanation as to how you arrived at your chosen answer. That really wasn't easy for me, when so much was done on a mixture of gut feelings and "pick a letter ... any letter" tactics.

One of the questions asked whether La Croisette in Cannes was a beach, a pier or a road. I'd been to Cannes. There was pretty much nothing there, so I decided that "road" was the best option. I pressed quickly enough for the rest of the team to actually believe I knew the answer, but I just wanted to try to put Paul under a bit of pressure if he was unsure.

Luckily, it was a road. Unfortunately, Paul wasn't fazed in the slightest ...

Somehow, I ended up one right answer away from making it back for the final chase, some four steps ahead of my white-suited opponent. It seemed almost too good to be true, and the gap quickly halved as Paul got two right in succession and I lost the knack of guessing correctly.

The next question concerned Dante's *Divine Comedy*, the 14th century poem that I've never read. The inscription "Abandon hope all ye who enter here" is supposed to appear at the entrance to: A) Heaven, B) Hell or C) Purgatory.

Hell, it must be Hell ...

Hang on, C sounds right too. Which one is it? I haven't a clue. Get this one wrong and he's only one step behind me. Oh no, what if I go out after being four steps in front? I'm going to look such an idiot ...

All those thoughts raced through my mind in a split second of genuine panic. Here was my dreaded fear of failure, and it was playing out for the nation to see one day. I convinced myself to stick with my original answer and take the consequences. I pressed B.

Brad laughed; he had obviously seen a reaction when "Hell" was unveiled, and the immediate hesitation and doubt caused by appearance of the third option. He gave the reveal the big build-up – those few seconds are awful – but then the word "Hell" on the screen (that was to my right and level with the Chaser) turned green; I was correct, and I was through.

Such a relief.

To be honest, once I was back in my seat, the nerves seemed to drain away. I had wanted to be part of the whole experience, and now I would be. It felt great.

Ash and Jess did their cash builder and after all four contestants had faced the Chaser, three of us were left with £20,000 in the proverbial "pot". (Notice how I haven't given away the one who didn't make it back ...)

Then came more water, more encouragement, and the reappearance of the independent adjudicator to oversee the selection of the set of questions for the final chase. A purple bag contained two ping-pong balls, one labelled A and one labelled B.

Set B was chosen.

We were then asked a few simple questions so that we could practise using the buzzers. I wasn't sure if mine actually worked, because the other two kept pressing theirs quicker!

Cue Brad and two minutes of questions. The score was displayed on an illuminated panel behind us, and it wasn't until we'd got to 15 points that I could see to my left how we were doing. We made it to 19 when the clock reached zero. We thought we'd done reasonably well, but were probably a couple short of a winning score. This opinion was echoed by the host and Chaser, although Paul conceded that the questions had been tough.

If you want to know what happened over the next couple of minutes, I'm afraid you'll have to watch the programme when it is eventually aired, but we were given no clue as to when that might be (apart from sometime in 2018).

Once the game was over, Brad shook each of us by the hand then headed back to his seat. The Chaser also left the set, and we actually never even got to meet Paul face-to-face, which was quite disappointing. We were escorted from the studio, as the next group was led in ... and at that point you realised *The Chase* was simply a conveyor belt, and that however it felt to be a one-off contestant, for everybody else in front of the camera and behind the scenes, it was just another day at work.

I'm so glad I took part in the show. It was another fascinating new experience to add to what, by then, had become a lengthy list, and I'm particularly pleased that Jess and I have stayed in touch.

I just hope to see, when the episode is eventually transmitted, that the cameramen managed to capture my best side!

CHAPTER 5

THERE GOES THE SPARE TYRE

PLAY BADMINTON AGAINST
AN ENGLAND INTERNATIONAL

In September 2015 I drove down to Milton Keynes to meet Rhys Walker, and play a couple of games of badminton against him. Rhys was England international, ranked number 4 in the country at the time. He was a multiple national age group champion, Commonwealth Youth and European Championship medallist ...

Maybe I should have just asked to have a coffee with him instead.

I'd never been to Milton Keynes before – the main reason being it's nowhere near Middlesbrough. They could have built this particular new town anywhere in the country, but chose to put it 220 miles away from where I live. Poor planning, if you ask me!

I hadn't swung a badminton racket in anger for a decade, and it took me quite a few hours just to find mine. Thankfully, despite the passage of time, the strings were all intact. Once I'd bought some trainers and borrowed a bag to put my kit in, I was officially ready for the off.

I did have a couple of concerns to mull over as I drove down to Buckinghamshire. Could I still hit a shuttlecock over a net, and how long would my hips keep me upright (let alone mobile)? I was fairly confident about the former, but although I suppose the latter will always be a worry, it was never going to stop me going out on court and giving it a real go.

I arrived slightly ahead of schedule and was sitting in reception when Rhys appeared. He had no problem recognising me – I was the only one in the whole complex who was old, unfit and holding a 20-year-old racket. We were able to have a short natter before I ventured into the impressive main hall. Rhys proceeded to tell me that the people looking at us, as I walked onto the bright green court, were in fact the majority of the England squad. Suddenly those 10 years seemed an absolute age!

Fortunately, when we knocked up, racket and shuttlecock connected ... most of the time. Rhys suggested that we play a few short games. We played first to seven.

At this stage, it is important to note that Rhys kindly made sure the points were competitive, but after the first couple of games, one thing was very apparent: I was even more out of condition than I imagined. But, on the plus side, there were one or two very brief glimpses of the old "Kirby magic"!

The fact that I lost all of our games was hardly a surprise, but although every score line started "Walker 7", there was actually one that ended "Kirby 6", and another "Kirby 5".

No one was more surprised than the portly, wheezing 51-year-old who was in desperate need of a rest and a drink after every couple of rallies.

During the breaks, and at the end of proceedings, Rhys and I had what I found to be an absorbing chat about the physical and mental demands of international badminton, the dedication and determination it takes to be an elite athlete, as well as the invaluable input of the team behind the scenes.

Looking remarkably athletic!

Sportsmen and women are essentially judged by their performances and results, but earning the right to compete takes unseen hours, days and months of preparation, fitness and skills work. You also have to be able to deal with the all-important psychological aspects of top-level sport (being able to manage nerves and produce optimum performance levels under intense pressure).

So often, small margins separate those in first place from those in second. And when two athletes are closely matched, Rhys explained to me, mental strength can provide that extra one per cent and make the difference between winning and losing.

For Rhys, being a top sportsman required him to move away from home. This meant he had to leave an embedded support network that had clearly been successful. This can't have been easy, but Rhys recognised that sometimes there were decisions and sacrifices that had to be made for the opportunity to progress to the next level.

Rhys clearly had a mature head on his shoulders to add to his talent and resolve. But as far as I was concerned, I had nothing left to give after 40 minutes. My legs were fine, but the old heart rate was getting faster and faster. Sometimes I guess you just have to accept that time has caught up with you.

That said, in among the occasional air shot and poor footwork, we had some enjoyable rallies, and a shot or two received a genuinely positive response from the other side of the net. What more could I have asked for?

This was undoubtedly one of the most memorable of all my challenges, but sadly what I thought was a stitch turned out to be quite an uncomfortable side strain. An athlete would tell you that the affected muscle group is known as the *latissimus dorsi*. But in my own terms, the pain that cost me a decent night's sleep was officially caused by a punctured spare tyre.

PLAY AN INTERNATIONAL ATHLETE AT HIS OR HER CHOSEN SPORT

One of the guests on the *Mentally Sound* radio show was a young lady called Jenny Wallwork, who had gone on the programme to talk about her own mental health experiences and her new charity, the Jenny Wallwork Foundation. The foundation offers practical advice and support to anyone struggling with mental illness. Alongside her work with the charity, Jenny was also working as an athlete mentor for the Dame Kelly Holmes Trust, an organisation that helps disadvantaged people get back into sport.

As a successful international badminton player, Jenny won Commonwealth silver and bronze medals and, at one stage, was ranked fifth in the world along with her mixed doubles partner Nathan Robertson. Yet, during her professional career, she fought a secret battle against bulimia – a truly horrible condition. Finally opening up to her parents must have been one of the hardest moments of her life, but it was very much a turning point for her.

I got in touch with Jenny because one of my challenges was to play an international athlete in his or her chosen sport. And although we'd not had a chance to meet on the radio, the connection was a good avenue through which to start a conversation. Jenny was really enthusiastic about the concept and aim of my challenges, and agreed to meet up when her work schedule brought her to the North East.

We met at Eston Leisure Centre (just two miles from my home) in April 2016. Jenny brought along James Kirton, a fellow athlete mentor and a swimmer of great distinction, who had represented Team GB at the 2008 Beijing Olympics.

If my worn joints weren't enough of a disadvantage, James revealed that he'd recently challenged Jenny to a game and been on the wrong end of a 21 – 0 drubbing, so it was with some trepidation that I lumbered onto the court.

The warm-up consisted mainly of me bending down to pick up shuttlecocks after swishing at thin air, but thankfully things improved (although it's all relative) when the "serious stuff" got underway – well, it was serious on my side of the net.

At the end of the first game (which I lost 21 – 13), Jenny commented that my height was a definite advantage – something that I felt was more than cancelled out by my age and lack of mobility. These were kind words, which I didn't fully appreciate at the time because I was on the verge of collapsing from exhaustion. My reactions were still reasonably good though, and I'd played one or two pretty decent shots along the way.

Jenny made sure that I worked really hard, and much as she didn't need to get out of first gear during our hour together, it was obvious that she was a superb athlete – her movement around the court was incredible. As you would have expected, she had every shot in the proverbial book, including a backhand that could reach the back of the court with ease, and a smash that even at half speed was hard enough to see, let alone try to return.

But just for the sake of good order, I sneaked into double figures in the second game. I then went on to lose the third game 21 – 14 … and loved every minute.

While those games against Jenny and Rhys were the only two badminton challenges on my list, I did take to the court one more time towards the end of 2016, at a charity badminton day in Garforth (near Leeds) which Jenny had organised.

The event gave ordinary folk like me the chance to face some of the country's finest players, all in aid of the foundation that bears Jenny's name. Olympic medallist Nathan Robertson was the highest-profile player in attendance, but also on view were others who'd tasted success in the Commonwealth Games, and plenty who had reached international level.

For the record I played three games of doubles – my partners being Kate Robertshaw (mixed team silver medallist in the 2014 Commonwealth Games in Glasgow), Sarah Milne (who had represented Team GB in the 2010 Youth Olympics), and Jenny herself. I won two games and lost one, although I seemed to be no more than an interested spectator for most of the matches.

I would say I've never seen a shuttlecock travel so fast, had I actually been capable of seeing it. I swear it was easier to hear it!

In between games, I spent quite a while chatting to Adam Whitehead, who was on DJ duty. Adam had also been an international athlete and a Commonwealth medallist, but his success had come in the pool and not on court, with gold in the 100m breaststroke in Manchester (2002). It was fascinating listening to not only his achievements, but also how difficult it had been to mentally adjust to life after elite competition.

It's easy to forget that once all the training, competition, trophies, medals and headlines have come to an end, life inevitably changes but continues in a new direction. I think it's important to recognise just how difficult that transition can be.

TAKE PART IN THE BOXING DAY
DIP IN THE NORTH SEA

There seems to be something of a tradition in this country that makes crowds of people head off to the coast the day after Christmas – with the sole aim of immersing themselves in freezing cold water. I couldn't see the attraction, but nevertheless I put it on my list of challenges.

I became less and less thrilled at the prospect as the day drew closer.

Redcar was the destination. It was a fairly chilly morning; overcast, but not raining, although in fairness it wasn't the temperature of the *air* that was really bothering me. There was a decent turnout, but I wasn't there for a social gathering. My sole aim was to get in and out of the icy North Sea without catching hypothermia.

I toyed with the idea of running into the water, but I was genuinely worried that the shock might cause a cardiac arrest! There's nothing like a moment of dramatic hypochondria!

In the end, I plumped for the leisurely wade and, yes, the water was absolutely freezing. As I got closer to Norway, so the waves gradually lapped over more of my body. By the time my chest disappeared, I was practically begging Elaine to take a couple of photos of me pretending to have a great time – so I could share them online for my noble mental health awareness cause, yes, but mainly so I could bring the ordeal to an end.

Moments later, I was heading back to the beach to thaw out ... challenge completed.

Was it a good idea? No.

Was I glad I'd done it? No.

Would I do it again? Have a wild guess!

SWIM A MILE

Although I had no intention of venturing back into open water, the fact that "swim a mile" was on the list meant that it was always going to be difficult to avoid dipping my toes into a chlorinated pool at some point. On the May Day Bank Holiday in 2017, I felt the time was right to go to my local leisure centre and see how close I could get to the 65 lengths of the 25-metre pool that would equal just over one mile. I had been doing quite a bit of training in the gym recently, so I knew I was reasonably fit, but an hour's breaststroke was a totally different proposition to the same time on a rowing machine. I was concerned that my back might seize up, but the hope was I would maybe get somewhere near halfway before the aches and pains started.

And as it turned out, it was around halfway when I got my first twinge – halfway down the second bloody length. Six lengths later, I was convinced one of my contact lenses had popped out (and yes, I know you're not supposed to wear them in the pool), but after a couple of minutes the blurred figures that kept overtaking me started to come back into focus, and all was well ... for a while.

I was even able to forget about my back ... when my neck and shoulders started to stiffen up. For a while I was genuinely worried I wouldn't be able to keep going, but as soon as I passed half way, I was confident that I was going to complete the mile.

The halfway point was a definite psychological barrier, but it turned out that I thrived on the knowledge that I had swum further than the distance I had left to go. I felt increasingly strong mentally, and finishing was simply a matter of *when*, not *if*. I didn't time myself to the split second, but as my weary arms touched the wall at the end of the 65th and final length, a quick look at the clock confirmed that it had taken a few seconds either side of 58 minutes to finish the task.

I relaxed for a few minutes before hauling my portly frame out of the water (at the first attempt – impressive!) then trudged slowly back to the changing room ... aching, but really happy that I'd completed another challenge – one that had posed both physical and mental barriers.

RACE AGAINST AN OLYMPIC SWIMMER

Calling this swimming challenge in 2017 a "race" is the ultimate misnomer.

My "opponent" (again in the loosest sense of the word) was Chris Cook, double Commonwealth gold medallist, Olympic finalist in the 4x100m relay in Beijing, and the first ever Briton to swim 100m breaststroke in under a minute.

I had contacted Chris through a mutual friend. I sent him details of what I was hoping to do, and explained why I was raising mental health awareness. When we spoke on the phone for the first time, Chris was really positive about the reasons behind my challenges. He seemed genuinely excited to be asked to get involved.

When you watch swimming on the television, it's hard to gauge just how fast the competitors are going because they're all quick. This challenge (scheduled for 100m at a pool in Darlington) was going to highlight the gulf between a genuine elite athlete ... and Chris.

Just kidding.

After several further phone conversations, it felt natural and easy when we actually met. I went and got changed, and made a mental note to breathe in as I strode confidently towards the pool. It had been nearly a decade since Chris's last Olympic adventure, but he still looked in great shape. I was also in perfect shape – had the shape in question been a space hopper.

We did a two-length warm-up – and I quickly realised I was already shattered!

There was an obvious need for a handicap. Chris suggested he should give me a full one-length start. I suggested he double it!

And so the scene was set. I would complete 50 metres, and as soon as my fingertips touched the wall at the end of my second length, Chris would set off.

I have never been a fast swimmer, but seeing as I had been training more than four hours a week on the rowing machine at the gym, I thought I might have a reasonable level of fitness. Even if I went flat out (again, it's all relative), I thought I might have been able to complete four lengths without stopping, needing oxygen or requiring any other medical intervention.

In truth, the writing was on the wall as soon as Chris joined the fray. It's hard to describe just how fast he was moving, but all I can say is that he was gliding, seemingly effortlessly, through the water. I wasn't even halfway down my final length when he took the lead, and I was almost 10 yards adrift when he finished.

I'm guessing it took roughly a minute for Chris to complete four lengths. In that time, I managed 40 metres.

There's not really much more I can say!

We stayed in the pool for probably 20 minutes afterwards, just chatting about various sporting experiences, shared acquaintances, and thoughts on mental health. From the perspective of an outsider, swimming looks like it is very much about the individual and can appear quite isolating, but it was interesting that what Chris missed most about being an international athlete was being part of a team, the camaraderie that helps to create those unforgettable memories and help you stay mentally healthy. That is a feeling that can translate to any level of almost any other sport. It also provides a shared experience between the elite and the amateur – allowing people like me and Chris to meet for the first time, yet talk as if we'd known each other for years.

Every challenge required a photo to show that I'd completed it. On the plus side, we didn't need a time-lapsed wide-angled shot to capture the end of the "race", but unfortunately Chris had just returned from a family holiday ... think tanned and toned next to pasty and portly!

On the way back to the car park, Chris mentioned Adam Peaty, the young man who was at that time the reigning Olympic, World, European and Commonwealth 100m breaststroke champion – and world record holder to boot.

When Chris swam sub-60 seconds in 2008, I believe it was one of the top 10 fastest times ever recorded for that distance, yet less than a decade later Peaty swam an incredible 57.13 seconds at the Rio Olympics. Two and three-quarter seconds might sound like no time at all (especially when I'd just been beaten by the swimming equivalent of a country mile), but if Adam and Chris had faced each other in their respective prime (notwithstanding what Adam may achieve in future), Adam would have beaten Chris by approximately 2.2 metres – a staggering margin given that medals can be decided literally by centimetres or fractions of a second.

It was fascinating listening to someone who had accomplished so much in the pool, and was an outstanding athlete in his own right, talk with such enthusiasm and genuine pleasure about the achievements of another swimmer.

As I reflected on the previous hour during the drive home, I was in no doubt that Chris had a natural gift to inspire. He was both thoughtful and insightful, and I just felt incredibly fortunate to have been able to spend some time in his company.

Later that evening, I uploaded the poolside photo and sent a message of thanks to Chris. Within a few moments, the thanks had been reciprocated:

It was brilliant to meet you and chat with you. It's such a great idea to capture people's attention about mental health by doing so many challenges. I feel privileged that you asked me to take part.

Genuinely humbling.

Chris also suggested he was getting slower with each passing year, so he didn't really want me to ask him for a second race in the pool.

Don't worry, Chris – I wasn't going to!

CHAPTER 6

A DIFFICULT DIAGNOSIS

Perhaps I need to offer some insight into the process that led me to recognise my specific condition for what it was.

By way of background, the term "dysthymia" was first used by a noted professor, Dr James Kocsis, as recently as the 1970s. As with any condition, there are a series of "official" symptoms, but given the mild and persistent nature of dysthymia, the sufferer may not be aware there is actually anything wrong.

And in that one sentence lies the fundamental problem with formally diagnosing dysthymia. How many people ring their doctor and ask for an appointment because they are feeling fine?

It's all obviously relative, but if we accept that someone feeling "fine" simply means they feel "normal" – i.e. how they've always felt – then the answer to this question should be something approaching zero. In my case, I essentially felt the same from my mid-teens right through to shortly before my 40th birthday. The way I felt seemed "normal" to me, and so I assumed I was fine. I didn't know that my "normal" actually wasn't fine at all.

But now, with hindsight and the right information, I'm able to be objective about my condition and accept that I was – and still am – prone to exhibiting *some* of the following symptoms associated with dysthymia:

- Gloominess

- Pessimism

- Humourlessness

- Inability to have fun

- Feeling passive and lethargic

- Introversion

- Feeling sceptical and hypercritical

- A tendency for self-criticism or being self-reproaching and self-derogatory

- A preoccupation with inadequacy, failure and negative events

Not everything in this list applies to me. I'm not humourless or incapable of fun, but there are many things in that list that I've dealt with for as long as I can remember.

What's interesting is that I never thought all those "negative" aspects of my personality were symptoms – they were just *me*. I thought they were just my personality traits. This was how I felt, day after day, year after year … it was all I knew. So why would I have sought medical advice?

There was a significant dip in my mood that led me to my visit to the GP's surgery. When I was diagnosed with depression I felt partly relieved at having an answer, an explanation for how I was feeling – but as I said, it still didn't seem quite right for me. As far as I was concerned, I was just feeling the same emotions I had always had, only far, far worse.

Interestingly, feeling like you're a deceiver is apparently another tell-tale sign of dysthymia.

As I mentioned in the Introduction, what I had was an episode of "double depression" – I had chronic dysthymia as standard, but also a case of depression on top of that, due to some traumatic life events. So even though I felt like a fraud, I had no reason to. I *was* depressed.

And once the "upper layer" (my depression) was treated and therefore removed, I would have described what remained (my dysthymia) as "normal". I thought that was job done. The doctor had treated my depression and its symptoms. But how could he have possibly diagnosed my personality traits?

Of course, I had no idea that dysthymia wasn't my "personality" at all, but an actual mental health condition.

After speaking for the first time about my mental health issues, I started to look at some elements of my personality – those that might be considered "classic" symptoms of depression – in much greater detail. My challenges were already underway at this point, and I was actively trying to raise mental health awareness. This meant that I was able to chat to a number of people working in the sector who had extensive knowledge and experience. And through those conversations, I began to self-analyse in even greater depth – until the day when everything finally (and wonderfully) slotted into place.

When I read about dysthymia, it was just like seeing me being described on a page. I felt a surge of adrenaline as the realisation dawned that this was what I had – what I'd always had. Perhaps it had been obvious to some or all the people with whom I'd spoken, but for me it had taken such a long time for all the pieces to fit together, that the moment was almost overwhelming.

I no longer felt like a fraud. What I had was real … and it had a name!

I began to replay random moments from my childhood in my head. Had I finally found an explanation for some of those distressing feelings I'd had, those I'd dismissed as "part of growing up"?

Nothing could change the past, but I was so happy that some of the more difficult emotional aspects of my teenage years had started to make sense.

You need to bear in mind that these are my experiences. Others may well have a different story to tell, but I do feel that dysthymia is an incredibly difficult condition to recognise and diagnose. That said, maybe heightened awareness of all aspects of mental health has led to greater understanding of dysthymia within general practice (and maybe patients generally have greater self-awareness?). I honestly don't know.

But when I reflect on how events have unfolded since 2004, I honestly don't think my doctor could have done more to support and treat me. I remain grateful to him to this day.

In hindsight, I realise now that the doctor hadn't only prescribed me the medication that allowed me to recover. He'd also helped me get well enough to truly think about my "traits" – or symptoms – more objectively. And that, for me, was crucial to so much that followed.

Researching and recognising my exact condition was a lengthy process, justified totally by the definitive and positive outcome. And it all stemmed from the massively important message that runs right through this book:

It's okay to talk, and it's fine to ask for help.

CHAPTER 7

EGRETS ... I'VE HAD A FEW

The subjects of this chapter are avine, equine and anguine (had to look that one up!). Basically, that means that these three challenge stories relate to a bird, a horse and a snake. I'm going to start with the third of the trio – one of the challenges I instantly regretted putting on the list.

HOLD A SNAKE

I don't have an irrational dread of snakes as such, I'm just not a big fan of things that slither ... and possibly bite. I wasn't exactly facing a deep-rooted, irrational fear, but I didn't fancy facing a rapidly widening jaw either. I was incredibly nervous, and so if my friends had been secretly hoping to see me enveloped by a 20-something-feet-long reticulated python, they were destined to be disappointed.

Way back in January 2014, I ventured into the reptile section of one establishment and explained what I was hoping to do. The shop did have quite a few snakes, and the animal that was chosen to be my photographic companion for the task was an adult corn snake (*Pantherophis guttatus*) measuring 5 feet in length.

There were one or two other candidates, but the dwarf boa (*Tightus squeezicus*) in the next tank gave me a look that simply said, 'Don't even think about it ...'

For the record, corn snakes are usually fairly docile, rarely bite and are blessed with attractive patterning that is hard to fully appreciate when you've got your eyes closed.

This particular snake was around four years old; in the wild they usually live for six to eight years, but can live considerably longer in captivity. I was encouraged to place one hand fairly near the snake's head (easier said than done!) and told that the snake would curl its body around my arm, which is pretty much what it did, leaving me feeling wary yet strangely curious in equal measures.

Its body was relatively thin, but certainly not without strength (the corn snake kills small prey by constriction). The skin was dry and smooth, not entirely what I'd expected, but apart from a couple of moments when its head turned and brushed against my hand, snake and human got on famously! The sense of relief was enormous.

Incidentally, at various stages during the book, you will come across some challenges that were completed more than once – this was never going to be one of them!

HAVE A BIRD OF PREY FLY ONTO MY HAND

Just a few weeks later I completed my next animal-related task at a nearby falconry centre, courtesy of the owner Colin Badgery and a very handsome golden eagle called Boris.

I'd carefully studied the weather forecasts in the lead up to the centre's opening weekend in 2014. The five-day forecast suggested Sunday would be fairly bright, but Saturday was likely to be cloudy. With that knowledge, we made the logical decision and arranged our visit for the Sunday. But, in typical British fashion, the forecast suddenly (and typically) swapped around. Saturday morning ended up being glorious, and there was rain in the air as Elaine and I got into the car the following morning.

Strong winds can pose more of a problem for birds if they're flying at relatively low levels, but thankfully, although it was overcast when we arrived, the rain had stopped and there wasn't too much of a breeze. Colin showed us the centre's largest birds – including white-tailed, bald and golden eagles, before being warned that one or two could get "feisty" – I'll assume it was just a coincidence that they were all females!

We also saw Ringo, the Eurasian griffon vulture. He was just three years old, but he weighed 19lbs and had a huge 9-foot wingspan. Ringo was having a bath when we passed him; he'd done his first ever public display the previous day and looked justifiably pleased with himself.

Evidently, vulture numbers in parts of Africa were dwindling because of the trade in ivory and rhino horn. Seemingly carcasses were being impregnated with poison, so that as soon as the birds came to feed, they were essentially doomed – all for the sake of a few pounds (or equivalent currency) for the poachers.

As it turned out, Boris was the bird with the responsibility of flying onto my hand, which by now was safely encased in a comfortingly thick glove. Boris weighed just over 6 pounds, had a 6-foot wingspan, and was 16 years old. (Apparently in captivity, the largest birds can live over 30 years – I just thought you might like to know.)

Colin expertly demonstrated what I needed to do. He placed a piece of raw turkey leg in the glove and gave a signal to Boris, who was perched on top of an aviary about 50 yards away.

Boris clearly wasn't impressed, and promptly flew off into the woods. I was briefly confused and worried that it'd gone wrong, but he returned a minute or so later and before I knew it, he'd landed on my hand and the food was gone. What I found particularly interesting was that Boris would plan his path to my hand by judging the speed and direction of the breeze. What an intelligent creature! The Golden Eagle is an amazing bird; it weighs next to nothing, but possesses so much grace, speed and power.

He flew to me twice more before "posing" for a few photographs. It was a fascinating, strangely quite emotional experience and I was absolutely enthralled at being in such proximity to a truly magnificent creature.

BE A RACEHORSE OWNER FOR A DAY

The mission to own a racehorse for a day took me two whole years to arrange. The reason behind my initial idea for the challenge was that I wanted to experience something new and exciting. But I also knew that arranging it would be quite a difficult thing to do, and I wanted a challenge that would test my emotional perseverance and patience.

Finally made it!

Essentially what I wanted to do was act as a racehorse owner for a day, which is far easier said than done. I'm indebted to Keith Nicholson, an old friend from my cricketing days, for his help in this challenge. Keith has a long-standing love of horse racing (matched only by his love of turning down numerous appeals for leg before wicket at many cricket grounds over the years). Keith's horse Dhaular Dhar, which he part-owned as a member of a syndicate, was declared for the 4:50 race at Ripon on 16th July 2016. And so finally Keith had the opportunity to invite me into the parade ring.

So many things had to slot into place for this task to be accomplished: the horse had to be declared to run at a course that was not too far from our respective homes, on a day when both Keith and I were free. Only so many members of the syndicate of owners could attend on any given day, so the next step essentially required mass unavailability of the other owners, so that we'd be able to attend.

Even then, we would be reliant on the weather. If the going at the racecourse was unfavourable, the trainer could pull the horse out of the race and we'd be back to the proverbial drawing board. We had several near misses along the way, but I did my best not to get frustrated. The possibility that it might happen always seemed to overshadow any disappointment when fate conspired against us, and I liked that I was able to keep such a positive outlook about the situation.

When the day came, it was a beautiful but slightly breezy afternoon, and thousands of racegoers had made their way to the picturesque North Yorkshire course. I met Keith and his good friend Colin Batey outside the entrance. We collected our owners' badges and headed for the Owners and Trainers bar, where I promptly spilt hot chocolate down my grey tie. *Bloody typical*, I thought, frantically wiping down my tie with a damp cloth. Thankfully, my pristine white shirt and new jacket avoided the chocolate dribble – I *almost* looked the part as we headed out to place our bets for the first race.

The favourite (and my selection) duly obliged, which meant that my bets for the next three races would be covered. This turned out to be quite a relief, since the next three horses finished second, second, and a distant last!

Each race was over in a matter of a minute or two and the afternoon flew by. It was great to catch up on some cricket chat after so many years and to explore the racecourse. I was also constantly surprised at how differently you were treated if you wore a red oval badge.

As the fourth race finished, we hurried over to the pre-parade ring to see jockey Carol Bartley bring in the 14-year-old Dhaular Dhar (known as "Dazzler" to his friends) for what would be his 150th race – quite remarkable. Keith said hello to Carol and had a quick chat with Jim Goldie Jr., son of the trainer Jim Goldie Sr. (which I presume you'd worked out for yourself!).

Carol, and a now saddled Dazzler, then did a few laps of the parade ring, where Keith, Colin and I were standing (I was trying – and failing – to look important). We took a few pictures before Jim joined us, and then the jockey Lewis Edmunds appeared. He looked very young … he *was* very young. In fact, Lewis was only three years older than the horse he was about to ride!

Lewis was an apprentice, which meant he could "claim" seven pounds, effectively giving the horse less weight to carry in compensation for the jockey's inexperience. The ground was ideal for the veteran campaigner, although Dazzler apparently wasn't keen on too much wind – well, there was one thing we had in common then. Lewis was instructed to get the horse comfortable towards the rear of the field and try to come with a late run that, if successful, would win me a small fortune.

I wished hard for that small fortune.

Moments later, Lewis was in the saddle and Carol (no mean jockey in her own right) led horse and rider out onto the course.

I must admit I began to feel a sense of nervous excitement as the horses cantered down to the start, were helped into the stalls and started the race. Perhaps all the effort of sorting out this challenge was going to pay off!

Sadly, despite both Dazzler and Lewis's best efforts, the next mile and a half didn't quite go according to plan. My hopes for a bumper payout and an early retirement were dashed.

We headed out onto the course to hear what Lewis had to say about the race. We managed to get a couple of photos (Keith taking mine without telling me to smile), before Dazzler disappeared to have some cooling water thrown over him, a bite to eat and a well-earned rest – the same three things I do every Saturday evening.

I bid Keith and Colin farewell before the final race to try to beat the crowd out of the car park. On the drive home I reflected on the afternoon's events.

As I said before, on the surface it had simply been the chance to enjoy a brand-new experience (and it *was* fantastic). But on another level, it showed the lasting effect of friendship. Keith and I hadn't seen each other in at least a dozen years, but he was still willing to do everything he could to turn this challenge into a reality. And when we did meet, we essentially picked up where we had left off (still no chance of an LBW decision). It just goes to show how powerful friendship can be in a person's life – whether it helps you to organise a seemingly impossible challenge, or helps you maintain your mental health. Or both.

As soon as I got home, I couldn't wait to upload some photographs and post a few thoughts about the afternoon on social media. Within minutes, Lewis Edmunds messaged me to say thank you for offering him the opportunity to ride Dhaular Dhar. It was a gesture that was as kind as it was clearly unnecessary, but it said a lot about the young jockey.

What a lovely way to round off a wonderful few hours.

CHAPTER 8

2B OR NOT 2B

There are members of my family who are really gifted and talented in various arts and crafts: my sister is a fantastic artist; my niece is arguably even better. My younger daughter can draw, paint, sing and act. My mum is great at making clothes, bags, jewellery – and, rather randomly, oven gloves.

I love to write, but I think it's fair to say that I wasn't blessed with many (if any!) creative genes. And yet that didn't stop me from having a go at painting, sketching, writing poetry, knitting and, er, baking (does that count? I guess it does).

SELL A PICTURE I HAVE PAINTED

One of the first challenges I attempted back in 2014 was to have a go at oil painting and to actually sell the finished article, with the proceeds going towards fundraising for charity. Actually, perhaps that should read "*any* proceeds" – the definite article presuming a level of interest that my lack of ability certainly couldn't guarantee.

To the best of my knowledge, this was the first time I had ever attempted painting in this particular medium, and although the aim wasn't to become the next big name in contemporary art (although it would have been a pleasant bonus), I just wanted to try my best and hope that the charitable cause might make the end result more appealing than the painting itself.

The subject was a sunrise I'd photographed outside a branch of a well-known supermarket chain the previous December, and I must admit I quite enjoyed mixing the colours to recreate the scene. The orange and yellow colours in the sky that winter morning were unusual but wonderful. I think I managed to preserve the unusual at least, and I found the act of adding paint to a cheap canvas substitute strangely therapeutic.

As soon as I started adding the trees, however, I realised that I couldn't paint trees. In the photo, the branches were thin and neatly defined, but in my version, they were pretty much the same width as the trunks. At this point, "strangely therapeutic" became "a tad frustrating".

Fortunately, I was able to remind myself that I was not exactly renowned for my artistic prowess, and my realistic opinion of the finished painting was that it actually didn't look too bad ... from a distance ... a long distance ... in the dark.

That said, it was still a major relief when I posted the painting on a well-known auction website, and the opening bid meant that Mind would benefit from a minimum of £1.99.

Here was the part that I needed help with: selling the finished piece. Over the next 10 days nearly 100 people visited the auction page, and my painting got a surprising 23 bids. When the listing ended, the highest bid was an incredible £20 – almost £20 more than I could ever have expected. Although I knew the "winner" (and I use this term advisedly), she asked to remain anonymous – presumably for fear that the painting might be targeted by the criminal underworld.

DRAW A PENCIL SKETCH

Three years elapsed before my next artistic challenge – this time it was to draw a pencil sketch. More accurately, it was a sketch of a sketch, a beautiful captivating work by Esther Burns entitled *Tear Face*, and I will admit that I was genuinely delighted with the finished picture. It took two and a half hours to complete and was my first and only attempt at recreating the original. I'd purchased a book with 30 pristine white pages, on the basis that the majority were likely to get scrunched up and hurled in the general direction of the nearest bin, accompanied by a tirade of expletives. But amazingly, I was left with 29 unused pages, and I didn't swear once!

The picture wasn't chosen at random. I wanted to find an image that in some way reflected the challenges' underlying theme of mental health awareness, and as soon as I saw the face and the single tear, I thought of Jodie … one of the two main protagonists in *The Beige Beetle*, my first and only novel.

Jodie was an 18-year-old student. She was funny, perceptive and caring, yet complex and vulnerable. She had suffered from bulimia throughout her teens, and while the physical effects were no longer obvious, mentally Jodie was still fragile. Jodie was an amalgamation of several people who had touched my life in some way, but some of her characteristics were entirely fictitious. I didn't know a great deal about bulimia, but some of Jodie's experiences mirrored those of a very good friend of mine, who talked about her life with this awful condition at length and in great detail. It must have been so hard to relive some of her genuinely harrowing moments, but this young lady's remarkable courage helped me to develop Jodie as a *person*, rather than simply a "character".

Back to the drawing. For me, the hardest part was getting the facial features correctly positioned and scaled in relation to each other (what I wouldn't have given for some tracing paper!), but I absolutely loved working on the eye and the mouth. Both areas were quite intricate and I wasn't sure I had the skill or the patience to make the drawing come to life. But when I stepped back, I was honestly taken aback at the result.

I now have a box of barely used pencils (6B to 4H, for any graphite aficionados) that are now residing in the loft after I called time on the briefest of artistic careers.

But it was really good while it lasted.

WRITE A POEM

My love of writing has never included poetry. If my memory serves me right, the last poem I read wasn't even in English. It was *The Aeneid* by Virgil – cue feeble attempt at a *Thunderbirds* joke ...

No, I'm going to be strong. That said, you can have 10 bonus points if you know Parker's first name.

The poem was one of four tasks added to the list after I received an email from Bryony Page, who had won a wonderful silver medal on the trampoline at the Rio Olympics. A couple of years earlier, Bryony had challenged herself to try 100 new or different things in 100 days. The stories made for great reading and it was only right that I pinched a couple of her ideas!

There are so many types or forms of poetry, and when I saw that one consisted of just three lines (haiku – bless you), I thought that would be perfect. But an even better idea was to take this challenge seriously and try to express in verse how dysthymia has affected my life. The poem's title represents both the random nature of mental illness, and also (in part) the free-form composition that follows. The "someone" is, of course, Elaine – and the conclusion is intended to reflect the amazing difference she has made, and continues to make, to my life – every single day.

And so, while writing a poem didn't involve me having to ask for help in this instance, I always kept in mind that Elaine had always been around for me, every time I *did* need help.

I have literally no idea whether these 21 lines are even remotely half decent, or just total rubbish. But I did give them a great deal of thought and found them very hard – both emotionally and to any degree of technicality – to write.

No Rhyme, No Reason

The reflection of the young man
Was blurred by tears
Cried alone because
No one could ever see
No one could ever know
No one would ever understand
Such overwhelming sorrow
And the pain inside a head
Held tight by an unseen hand
That refused to release its grip.
The reflection of the older man
Now blurred by passing years
And fallen tears
Cried together because
Someone saw
Someone knew
Someone wanted to understand
A mind that fears the future
Yet is haunted by the past
But a man who won't give up the fight
Against that unseen hand.

I will leave the final word on this brief poetry segment to Lady
Penelope Creighton-Ward's faithful butler and chauffeur: 'My name
is Aloysius, m'lady.'

CREATE A MOTIVATIONAL PICTURE

This was also one from Bryony's list. It sounded straightforward, but it took almost two hours to find the right quote and a photographic concept that matched the words.

Social media is overflowing with so many quotes and sayings covering almost every imaginable aspect of life, so I suppose that picking just one that had a strong personal resonance was always going to take a bit of time – especially if I was to take the task seriously. Eventually I found a couple of lines that really hit home. The quote was attributed to the author George Eliot, and read thus:

It is never too late to be what you might have been.

George Eliot was the pen name of Mary Ann Evans, the noted author of *Middlemarch*, *The Mill on the Floss* and a number of other novels I've never read. The former was set in the fictional weaving village of Tipton, but was actually based on the Foleshill area of Coventry – where many of my mother's ancestors lived and worked during the 18th and 19th centuries. It was a compelling link between me, George Eliot, and her powerful words.

The finished article featured the quote superimposed over a picture of the sun trying to break through dark clouds (all very symbolic). It also comprised three photos of me, all at different ages.

When I initially looked at the three versions of my face, all I saw were my failings and mistakes. Initially I found no joy in this reflection of myself. This hardly fulfilled the motivational aim of my challenge.

I was also quite nervous about posting the picture online in case anyone thought the exercise was somehow self-indulgent. As it transpired, the picture received very little reaction (on the plus side, that meant no negative response), but it was a worthwhile exercise in the end because the words, at least, did resonate with me.

I do still look at the photo from time to time, and the words continue to hit home.

Hopefully, one day, I will finally see the face of someone who didn't always get things right. I will see someone who kept going, never gave up, and maybe – just maybe – got close to being what he might have been ...

CHAPTER 9

FERRY CROSS THE MURSEY

VISIT A FOOTBALL GROUND IN NORTHERN IRELAND, SCOTLAND, ENGLAND AND WALES IN ONE DAY

I've only afforded one task an entire chapter of its own, and it was my 99th challenge. It was undoubtedly one of the biggest undertakings of the whole four years: to visit a football ground in all four home nations in one day.

The challenge was actually the brainchild of Keith Nicholson, the man who had been instrumental in arranging for me to be a racehorse owner for a day in 2016. I thought it was a belting idea. Keith initially suggested that he might come along as navigator / photographer, but when a date was eventually agreed – summer's day in 2017 – Keith immediately booked a sunshine holiday with his good lady and declared himself unavailable!

Undeterred, I began to plan a provisional route around clubs that (according to the map, at least) weren't too far off the beaten track. The most obvious obstacle was the Irish Sea, but with the Cairnryan ferry terminal being just a few minutes' drive away from Stranraer FC's Stair Park, that seemed the most sensible Scottish ground.

There were several clubs located in Belfast, so that just left England and Wales.

The latter was a pretty straightforward choice. If it wasn't Wrexham, it would be a bloody long trek down to the likes of Cardiff and Swansea – and I still had to get home afterwards. For the English club, I plumped for Wigan Athletic. There were a few possible candidates close to the M6, but an old friend (and former Gateshead Thunder rugby league coach) Steve McCormack was working for Wigan Warriors rugby league club. As it turns out, they shared the DW Stadium with their footballing counterparts. My initial hope was that I would get a chance to catch up with Steve.

Given the distance and the time constraints, I had to start in Belfast with a stop-off at Glentoran FC (on the advice of a couple of my friends), before catching the early ferry to Scotland. The crossing would take roughly two and a half hours – and we had to arrive at the terminal at least an hour before departure. But once Stranraer FC had been ticked off, it would then be a case of pointing the car south and starting a minimum four-hour trek to Wigan. The last leg to Wrexham totalled less than 60 miles, but the slower roads meant it would still take at least another 90 minutes.

And I still had to get home afterwards ...

Allowing for a 10-minute stop at each ground and given a consistent run of luck with the traffic (as well as no problems with the car), I estimated the whole day would take something in excess of 15 hours.

I wanted to make the trip in the middle of the year to ensure as much daylight as possible (vagaries of the British weather notwithstanding). And, as it happened, Elaine and I were on leave for two weeks in June and would have a couple of free days after returning from a well-earned holiday. Deciding to do the event on Friday 23rd June gave me the time to get to Belfast on the Thursday and still have the weekend at home before having to go back to work.

It was at this point that Elaine decided she would come with me. I hadn't wanted to put her in a position where she felt obliged to spend a day in a car with her husband, but the offer of a trip to the Titanic Museum in Belfast (a city neither of us had visited), and the promise of a large bag of mint humbugs were enough to tip the balance.

I had contacted all four clubs in advance to see if there was much interest in the challenge. I think it's safe to say that unfortunately there wasn't, but Steve McCormack went out of his way to make sure we'd get the chance to take photos pitchside at the DW Stadium. And I did get a reply from Wrexham to confirm that we wouldn't be able to access the ground, as the Racecourse Stadium was due to host an Olly Murs concert the following evening. Fortunately, all that was necessary to complete the task was the ability to take photos outside the stadium.

I also received a message from the Glentoran secretary, offering to show us round the ground on the Thursday evening. I gratefully accepted ... and never heard another thing about it!

So anyway, at five o'clock on the morning of Thursday 22nd June, we left Middlesbrough for the west coast of Scotland to catch the lunchtime ferry across the Irish Sea. A quick calculation confirmed that the total distance we'd have to drive (door to door) would be something like 660 miles – my challenge was to be behind the wheel for the whole time we were on the road.

The trip to Cairnryan was uneventful, but the scenery was beautiful. The first 210 miles went without a hitch. But even though I knew the driving would be a bit of a test, I hadn't expected to recreate an *actual* driving test. When we were directed onto the ferry, a camera-carrying tourist darted right in front of the car, just as I was pulling away. The steward and Elaine both yelled and I instinctively slammed on the brakes. The emergency stop was successfully completed, and the tourist was angrily dispatched back to her coach by the steward.

We were the first car onto the deck – and would therefore be at the front of the queue to leave the ship in Belfast. We were shown where to park – it was on the ramp, on an uphill slant, with another vehicle no more than a foot behind me. That didn't feel too promising, and as we left the car and headed for the lounge (as they called it), I knew I'd be faced with a hill start in a car I wasn't really used to, with a guaranteed thud (and insurance claim) coming if I missed the bite and rolled backwards. No pressure, then ...

I have to say the ferry was amazing. The crossing was calm, the lounge really comfortable, and there was complimentary wine for the lady. If I'd known that, I wouldn't have bothered buying the humbugs ...

When the moment came to disembark, the hill start went like a dream – much to my enormous relief. We were first off the ferry ... and last out of the port, after the sat-nav decided to pack in. We finally found the hotel and had a pleasant visit to the museum, before an early night in preparation for another five o'clock start the next morning.

First stop was Glentoran FC, just a mile or so from the hotel. When we found the ground, there were signs saying that the area was being used by a film crew. That explained why the words "Manchester City" were painted on the wall. The production must have been set in the "good old days", because the prices above the turnstiles were all in shillings.

When we got to the gate, it was wide open. We strolled in, only to be confronted by a security guard who asked if he could help.

Spoiler alert: he didn't.

'We are doing a tour round all the four home nations in a day to raise mental health awareness, and just want to take a photograph ...'

'I can't let you in, so I can't.'

'It's quarter past five in the morning. We've travelled from North East England to get here, and it'll only take 30 seconds ...'

'I can't let you in, so I can't.'

'We've even got an email from the secretary …'

I think you can guess the next bit, so you can.

Elaine was philosophical; I wasn't happy at all. But I knew this day wasn't going to be easy. We got the best picture we could from the street, and set off for the ferry terminal.

The crossing back to the mainland was enjoyable, possibly because we had a massive breakfast which set us up for the majority of the day. The trip to Stair Park took no time at all, and once again the views were wonderful. Stranraer FC was duly ticked off – two down, two to go.

It took quite a while to reach the English border due to the volume of lorries on the predominantly single lane A77, but after joining the M6, we decided to have a quick stop and fill up with petrol – for the record, the unleaded petrol was a scandalous 20p per litre more expensive than our local supermarket.

Eventually we trundled into Wigan and found the DW Stadium – an impressive-looking arena. We were escorted out onto the pitch and Elaine showed off her photography skills. That was about as much as we had time for, before heading back into the car and onwards to Wales …

As we got closer to our fourth and final destination, the lack of service stations only heightened the need for a toilet stop. In the end, we found a huge garden centre just off the main road about 5 miles from Wrexham. Elaine thought there might be some time and an opportunity to browse. Suffice it to say, she was mistaken.

The Racecourse Stadium was fairly easy to spot, but parking proved a bit more troublesome. We ended up in what I think was a college or university campus, but after a short walk and a click of the shutter, the challenge was nominally completed.

The time was a quarter to five … 14.5 hours after I'd forced that smile outside Glentoran's ground. There was still plenty of activity going on in preparation for the following evening's concert, and I thought now would be a really good time to include some sort of pun using the title of an Olly Murs song ...

An excellent plan, with one major flaw: I don't think I know the title of any of his numerous (I'm guessing) hits.

Never mind. We strolled back to the car and when I switched on the engine, I looked at the milometer. It read 500.2 miles.

Olly Schmolly ... what about The Proclaimers?!

I resisted the temptation to break into song. After all, we were still over 160 miles from home. It started to rain as we headed north, but thankfully it drizzled more than it poured, and the traffic wasn't too heavy considering it was the end of the working week. We stopped at Birch services on the M62 to avoid the worst of the congestion, and emerged to a clearer road and much brighter skies.

We eventually pulled up in our drive shortly before nine o'clock. It had been a long, and at times exhausting, day, but the company had been fantastic, and the mood had been mostly upbeat ever since we'd boarded the ferry to Cairnryan.

I'd been really worried in advance about the possibility of delays, but the traffic and the roads were actually fine (apart from just a couple of slow stretches). I was so relieved that during the day, I'd never been in doubt that we'd complete the task.

Had I been on my own though, I'm sure I would have struggled more with the effects of fatigue. But having Elaine with me made a huge difference. I felt a very definite sense of achievement at having completed a tough challenge that had been suggested by someone else (and Keith duly sent his congratulations from his sun-drenched Italian retreat). I flopped onto the sofa for a long overdue and much-needed glass of vino, and as soon as I took my first sip, all the events of the previous hours suddenly felt totally surreal.

Just so you know, alcohol after a long drive is a really bad idea – it goes straight to your head, you start feeling a bit fuzzy, and then (wait for it ...) your heart skip, skips a beat ...

CHAPTER 10

THIS IS HOW IT FEELS

I think it's important to try to put into words how it actually *feels* to have a form of mental illness and reflect on how the condition has affected my adult life.

Right from the outset, I want to point out that dysthymia, while chronic, is also relatively mild. What follows is, therefore, arguably the tip of the proverbial iceberg, should you perhaps be reading this to understand the possible effects of (and the consequent daily struggles with) more serious depression, bipolar disorder, schizophrenia, borderline personality disorder, anorexia or bulimia (nervosa) ... and so the list continues.

Every morning, I wake feeling flat. Not some, or most, mornings ... *every* morning.

Even on a good day, it still feels like my head is being held tightly by a giant hand. The exact definition of a "not so good" day depends very much on how tightly the hand chooses to squeeze.

I readily accept I have little reason to feel low. I have a wonderful wife (an understatement), a loving family, plenty of friends, a nice home, a good job and reasonable health for an old bloke with dodgy hips. There will be some of you who can't understand why I don't spring out of bed and skip down the stairs every single morning (hips notwithstanding). And to an extent I agree.

But do you not think that, if it was that easy, I'd have experienced a daily rush of inner happiness upon waking, at some point during the past four decades?

Dysthymia does not necessarily give you the exaggerated highs and lows that come with other conditions. It just basically makes "normality" that much gloomier.

But when you've known no different, and feeling low and flat and head-squeezy is "normal" to you, then it's perfectly reasonable to assume that you should just get on with it – because … well … that's what everybody does.

I was probably quite distressed when I first started to feel unexplained, profound sadness during my teens. But the more it happened, the more I amended my definition of "normal" and just accepted the tears. Actually, I didn't just accept them … I would almost go out of my way to encourage them. I wanted to cry … I *needed* to cry … and so I would find a quiet corner and think about literally anything (real or imaginary) that would make me keep crying until the giant hand finally loosened its grip.

In the intervening years between then and the onset of my depression (more than a quarter of a century), I continued to experience irrational periods of desolation. Dark thoughts always came along for the ride. I reached a point where the negative side of my personality was so dominant that I almost functioned "better" when I felt overwhelmed by sorrow.

My "normal" then shifted yet further. Dysthymia became overshadowed by depression. Dark thoughts become commonplace … compulsive … and occasionally genuinely compelling. Part of me knew something was wrong, but I simply wasn't strong enough to fight, let alone overcome, my demons (if that's the right word). In truth, the stronger part of me didn't want to fight … I believed I deserved to feel the way I did.

It was a potentially dangerous downward spiral. And as much as I tried, whether instinctively or deliberately, to hide what I thought was simply a weakness rather than an illness, those who cared most about me could see through the charade.

Eventually, I crumbled, almost certainly tipped over the edge by the pressure of trying to deal with a series of events that eventually led to the end of my first marriage. There are circumstances surrounding that that are too personal to go into, but suffice it to say it was a distressing time in my life.

Luckily, that single phone call to the doctor was the first step to getting to where I am today.

I must admit to feeling guilty sometimes. There are people who deal with what I would consider far worse events than the breakdown of a marriage, and yet somehow find the strength to keep going. I can't believe that anyone reaches their fifties without experiencing one or more major trauma in their adult life, be it bereavement, serious illness, marital breakdown, redundancy, etc. Experiencing the symptoms I have, when all is seemingly well with the world, is difficult to deal with and quite hard to justify (if only to my emotional self) when I consider how many obstacles other people have to overcome.

But I have to remind myself that as far as stress and anxiety are concerned, there are numerous potential triggers. Mental illness can also rear its head without any warning. There is no real advantage to comparing. It serves no useful purpose.

Dysthymia is a persistent and insistent adversary, and that first drip of negativity can easily develop into an overwhelming deluge. Looking back at the past 30-or-so years, I can see that there is no pattern to my low moods. And on those rare occasions when I've experienced more severe symptoms, there wasn't always an obvious reason or trigger. I used to spend ages trying to rationalise how I felt and find that elusive explanation, but over time I've learnt to just accept the "bad days" and conserve my emotional energy and strength. I need to use it to fight my negative thoughts, rather than expend it on pointless self-analysis.

At least, that's what I try to do!

As if to confirm dysthymia's somewhat random nature, I would say that the worst single episode I had in the past three decades was that episode in the hotel room in Birmingham in 2011. At that time I was settled in Middlesbrough and happily married to Elaine. Maybe I've been worse at various stages in my adult life, but have somehow found a way of blanking out the memories. Or perhaps I wasn't as aware of myself before then. Either way, it doesn't really matter.

I can see the irony in the fact that one of my lowest points was during my happiest years. I don't actually need to understand why. I just need you to understand that you don't need to be at your lowest or weakest to be affected by mental illness.

Dysthymia is still very much a part of me – and probably always will be. But while I'm affected by it every day – to a greater or lesser degree – every day is not defined by dysthymia. It might not sound much of a difference, but I can assure you that it absolutely is.

CHAPTER 11

BRIEF ENCOUNTERS

FIND SOMEONE WITH THE SAME DATE OF BIRTH AS ME

As you will soon discover, a number of my challenges revolved around meeting someone. Often it was someone reasonably well known (to make things harder for myself and spread my mental health message around influencers) but the list also included a couple of lengthy strolls down memory lane. Another task was to find someone with whom I shared my exact date of birth.

I initially thought that this was going to prove really difficult (the famous Birthday Paradox only applies to a date, not the year as well), but somewhat bizarrely it turned out to be one of the first challenges I completed back in 2014. So that's where I'm going to start ...

I had only found two celebrities who entered the world on 3rd June 1964: the handsome actor James Purefoy and Kerry King, the much-tattooed and slightly less handsome guitarist in the heavy metal band Slayer. However, it turned out that by a happy coincidence, someone else who shared my birthday not only worked for the same organisation (NHS Blood and Transplant), but worked in the same planning and marketing department as me!

While I was based in Newcastle at the time, Gillian Meston worked in Leeds (although the two teams did know each other reasonably well). And although it probably seems remarkable that out of a total of no more than 20 staff across the two sites, two people would be born on the same day, there were actually two other members of the Leeds team who also shared the same date of birth (in 1984). The odds against such a coincidence happening twice in a small group must have been astronomical.

Gill and I were born only 25 miles and 15 minutes apart. Gill appeared (if that's the right word) first at half past six in the morning. Basically, that meant that while the Collins family were celebrating the safe arrival of their daughter at their Leeds home, my mum was still pushing for all she was worth over in York's Fulford Maternity Hospital.

During one of my reasonably regular visits to the Leeds office, Gill and I posed for the mandatory challenge-completing photo, and disappointingly (from my perspective), Gill looked roughly 15 years younger than me, rather than 15 minutes older. In my defence, I hadn't had time to shave and had driven 60-odd miles at some unearthly hour in the morning – and I reckon with a later start and less facial hair I could easily have got the gap down to something approaching single figures.

MEET AN OLYMPIC GOLD MEDALLIST

For as long as I can remember, I have been captivated by the Olympic Games – so many sports, so many incredible athletes and stories. My favourite ever moment in individual Olympic competition dates from the year I was born – 1964 – and concerns the women's 800-metre race (one of the most incredible races you will ever see). I don't really have any "heroes" as such, but the winner of the gold medal for that particular event in Tokyo is someone for whom I have a huge amount of admiration.

Her name is now Ann Brightwell, but back in October 1964 she was Ann Packer. What follows is a short part of a fascinating phone interview she gave me in early 2015.

One Olympic gold medallist ... and me.

In all, I actually ran six races in six days, but I didn't feel physically tired, because I was extremely fit. I trained probably harder than any woman had trained in that era. I was doing weights and sometimes training three times a day, all on top of having a full-time job. As well as being in really good physical condition, I was unwittingly perfectly prepared for the 800 metres, but I didn't realise it at the time. I was a sprinter who hadn't been good enough at sprinting, and that's why I stepped up to the 400m. I'd got into the European team two years earlier in the 200m; I reached the final, but I was never going to be a world beater at the sprints. I moved up in distance on the recommendation of my coach, Dennis Watts, and Robbie [Brightwell, Ann's fiancé at the time] who was obviously an established 400-metre runner.

Psychologically it was very difficult because I was still disappointed about my sprinting. Robbie's race hadn't gone according to plan either. Although my first heat time in the 800-metre race wasn't particularly good, I got through it.

To be honest, I wouldn't even have been able to tell you what the 800-metre world record was. I was in the race because there was a space. Dennis Watts had made me run a time trial over 600m before we went to Tokyo, just for endurance work, and he was quite astounded by the time that I did. I ran two 800s, again to build up my stamina.

One was at Leyton and the other at White City, and I managed to get the Olympic qualifying time. I said I wouldn't do the event in Tokyo if it was going to interfere with my 400m race, but as luck would have it, it didn't. The event started the very next day after the 400m finished, so I had nothing to lose by giving it a shot. I wasn't taking anybody's place, so it was just a peculiar set of circumstances that found me running in the 800-metre race.

It sounds very simplistic, but people kept telling me that if the other girls ran the first lap in about a minute, that would be very close to their best 400m time. Normally these girls would run 800m, 1,500m or even cross country. But since I was an ex-sprinter, a quicker pace would have been perfect for me. The girls actually went through the first 400m in under 60 seconds in the final, which was really pushing it for them. I knew that if I could stay with them in the third 200m stretch and was still in touch coming off the final bend, then I would have a great chance of winning. Most of them just wouldn't have that basic sprinting speed.

I know it looked like I was quite a way behind, but I felt very comfortable. With about 200 metres to go, I was near the back of the pack. But it was a single group, so I never felt out of the race. I was actually watching the New Zealand girl Marise Chamberlain, because after me, she was the fastest 400-metre runner in the race. She didn't compete in the event in Tokyo, but she had been a 400-metre runner in the past and had more basic speed than the others. So, when she stepped out of the group and went for it, that was when I made my move. The French girl [Maryvonne Dupureur] was always a front runner – I didn't know that, but obviously I found out that she always ran from the front, and very successfully. But after running wide round the last bend, I overtook her coming down the final straight as I made my final effort for the tape.

The Japanese officials were organised brilliantly. As soon as you'd finished your event, they'd appear carrying the box with your tracksuit in, and you'd be escorted straight off the track. But Robbie had managed, along with the rest of the relay team, to somehow persuade the officials to let them stay near the finish, because his fiancée was running in the next *race (which, luckily, was straight afterwards). So that's how he came to be there, but I didn't know until I'd finished, and then I saw them. There was John Cooper, Robbie, Adrian Metcalfe, Tim Graham and Milkha Singh, who was a friend of Robbie's. I'd met him in a lift inside the stadium just before the race and he'd said to me, 'You will win!'*

If you win a race nowadays, there are all sorts of ways you can celebrate. Someone will throw you a flag, and you do a lap of honour. But in those days you didn't do anything like that. So to have someone there to share the moment – with the boys pointing up at the screen saying, 'You've broken the world record!' – was fantastic!

Little did I realise during our conversation that I would not only be offered the chance to meet Ann in person, but that I would actually be invited to her Cheshire home for a chat over tea and biscuits (in November 2015).

You've just read part of the remarkable story behind Ann's Olympic success, and to put the medal into some sort of context, British women have won just 10 individual track-and-field golds in the whole history of the modern Olympic Games. Mary Rand started the proverbial ball rolling a few days before Ann won her gold medal. The other eight are: Mary Peters (Pentathlon, 1972), Tessa Sanderson (Javelin, 1984), Sally Gunnell (400m hurdles, 1992), Denise Lewis (Heptathlon, 2000), Kelly Holmes (800m and 1500m, 2004), Christine Ohuruogu (400m, 2008), and Jessica Ennis (Heptathlon, 2012).

So, it was with a mixture of excitement and nerves that I made the trip across the M62, M60, A627, A34, etc. The weather was miserable, but the journey was fine – except for a crack on my windscreen that emanated from a chip that must have happened early on in proceedings. The crack grew to about six or seven inches in length but thankfully got no worse, although a call to a certain well-known glass replacement service was required when I got home.

It was always going to be a slightly surreal moment when I knocked on the Brightwells' front door (bouquet of flowers in hand), but after that initial meeting Ann and I sat in her kitchen and chatted away for something like an hour and a half, barely pausing for breath. Ann's husband Robbie popped in a few times – and their three medals also made an appearance.

It was a wonderful experience. Spending time in Ann's company was the very definition of a pleasure and a privilege. It was a fantastic new experience, and a day I will never forget.

MEET A MEDALLIST FROM LONDON 2012

One of the challenges on the original list was to meet a medallist from London 2012. It took a fair bit of arranging, but in the end, I was able to meet not one medallist, but five, back in March 2014.

It was always going to be a long day, but it turned out to be a very (maybe even very, very) long day. I spent nine hours out of the house, eight and a bit of those in the car during a round trip of 373 miles. My destination was Leicester Grammar School, the event being a hugely important clash between the Leicester and Reading ladies' hockey teams. But the real reason I was going was an opportunity to meet members of the GB Olympic squad who had won that bronze medal at London 2012.

My sporting prowess (limited as it was) lay on a cricket field, but I played a fair bit of hockey at school – there were only muddy and bumpy pitches back then. I did have a reasonable goal-scoring record in inter-school matches, although it became less impressive when you took out the deflections past our own goalkeeper! I was once accused of playing hockey like a cricketer, an inference I angrily rejected by pushing a free hit through square leg for four ...

The progress of the women's GB Olympic squad at London 2012 was compelling, but a heartbreaking semi-final defeat to Argentina left the team needing to beat New Zealand to secure the bronze medal. The game was goalless at half time, but then they scored three goals in fairly quick succession in the second half, all from penalty corners. This had given the girls an unassailable lead.

The intense disappointment of the previous game was replaced by elation as the reality of their collective achievement sank in.

It was a brilliant moment, but before we could meet some of those involved in person, Elaine and I had to actually get to the hockey game in Leicester.

Our trek south was slowed by constant speed restrictions, stopped altogether by a bloody traffic jam, and pleasantly interrupted by a live interview for BBC Radio Leicester, which was conducted on a side road just off the M1 near Denby Dale.

We finally arrived at the school and found the pitch (not muddy and not bumpy), the best part of five hours after we'd left home. There were less than 10 minutes of the game remaining and the score was 2–1 in favour of the visitors. That's how it stayed.

I'd made arrangements to meet, and be pictured with, the two Leicester players and the three from Reading who had been members of the GB Olympic squad. The only problem was that Nicola White and Hannah MacLeod had literally just finished on the losing side in a vital game, and even though they knew I was coming, I felt sure the last thing they wanted to do was stand with some old bloke they'd never met before and smile for a camera.

But they were lovely. They chatted away, and even brought along their medals for me to see – and put round my neck. The medals were surprisingly heavy and it was so kind of them to set aside their understandable disappointment to help make the day so memorable.

I then had the chance to talk with Reading's Alex Danson, Emily Maguire and GB captain Kate Richardson-Walsh. In the picture, I was actually wearing Alex's medal, which had somewhat incongruously emerged from a sock thrown down from the balcony!

It might have only lasted 20 minutes out of nine hours, but it was a pleasure to meet five young women who were among the elite in their chosen sport, and who had already accomplished so much.

The fact was that for four of them, the best was yet to come with Team GB's amazing gold medal in Rio 2016.

TRACK DOWN A CLASSMATE FROM MY FIRST SCHOOL

I'm now going to look back at the day I met the woman who, well over 40 years earlier, had been a primary school classmate (the nominal part of the challenge), as well as also being my "first love" (the embarrassing revelation).

Towards the end of May 2014, Elaine and I headed south to the pretty little North Yorkshire market town of Helmsley, to meet Sarah Corden-Lloyd (née Wombell) – a contemporary at York College between 1968 and 1972. I had been anxious the previous evening. We had exchanged emails and texts since I managed to get in touch with her back in the January, but actually meeting her was something else altogether. We may have been childhood sweethearts (when we were seven) but the intervening decades meant we were essentially strangers.

We had arranged to meet at a coffee shop. Elaine and I arrived first – which was a surprise seeing as you needed a bloody degree to operate the parking meter – but just a couple of minutes later a face that was more familiar than I had anticipated appeared at the other end of the shop. I suppose any level of familiarity came from the fact I knew I was going to see her; on any other day Sarah could have walked right past me and I'm pretty sure I wouldn't have recognised her. She looked really well though. She still had the same lovely eyes that had made such an impression all those years earlier.

As it turned out, I needn't have been nervous; the introductions and conversation were relaxed and natural, and there wasn't a single awkward moment – well, apart from feeling my cheeks start to redden as Sarah related a Valentine's card story from c.1972 ...

I suppose we cross paths with so many people during our lives; in most cases those paths inevitably head off in different directions and never converge again. The fact that Sarah and I attended the same primary school was basically all we had in common, and was no real basis for adult friendship. We spent a couple of very enjoyable hours in her company, heard about Sarah's life and family and shared our own experiences and stories. Maybe our respective paths will converge again one day, maybe they won't. But even if it was just the once, I'm glad they did.

A few days later, I reached my half-century. On the eve of my 50th birthday, I penned some thoughts in response to a question Sarah had posed during our chat: was I a fatalist?

The day before a milestone birthday had to be the perfect time for introspection, so I'm going to remind myself – and tell you – that the answer is yes ... to a point.

Strictly speaking, I would presume that belief in fate implies that we have no ability to influence the future, and, by definition, our own actions. We do what we do because we were always "fated" to do so.

My understanding is that if every event is causally determined – by a "God" in whatever form – then that is, strictly speaking, determinism. Fate does not require a "cause" for things, as such – just an inevitable outcome.

But if our actions and consequent outcomes are all pre-determined, I would find it hard to reconcile things that I class as morally wrong. For example, could a murderer reasonably claim that they could not be responsible for their actions that were, theoretically, unavoidable?

For me, there just has to be an element of free will in the decisions or choices that we make. Even if free will simply relates to a person's ability to have some control over their own conduct, to choose between what is considered morally (or ultimately legally) right and wrong. That seems to be a more logical notion. At least then there can be no issue with accountability for the actions we take.

From a religious perspective, I class myself as agnostic. I absolutely accept there *could* be some divine power that controls us, our world and beyond, but I do not know it to be true. It is perhaps that lack of knowledge or understanding that allows me to believe that we do have some freedom in the actions and decisions we take – even if they simply guide us towards our ultimate destiny. If there is no free will, then what is the actual point?

The determinist would consider that the actions of the past, coupled with the laws of nature, absolutely decide the future. The fatalist might shrug his or her shoulders and accept the inevitable, but include the concept of free will and you have compatibilism (the idea that fatalism and determinism can coexist).

The end might still be inevitable, but at least you have the freedom to choose the path(s) you take.

I accept that this standpoint is the equivalent of straddling the philosophical fence, but it's where I prefer to sit. Compatibilism seems a contrary concept, but it offers justification; and even some element of comfort to this deep thinker.

That's where I left it in June 2014, and that's where I'm going to leave it now. If you thought I couldn't do highbrow, hopefully I've proved you wrong.

MEET SOMEONE WHO HAS HAD A TOP 10 SINGLE

Now for a musical interlude, and an encounter with someone who, at one time, was reputedly the biggest variety star on the planet ...

The challenge had been to meet someone who'd had a top 10 single. The official charts began back in 1952, so by definition there were hundreds and hundreds of artists who had recorded songs which had reached those heights. Sadly, the number of those people I actually knew totalled roughly none.

So, to try to narrow down the search I decided to do two things: look at all the upcoming concerts /gigs / shows (delete depending on your age) to see who might be appearing in the North East, and – rather randomly – the second was to see how many singers or musicians shared my birthday – which, to remind you, and specifically from a present-sending perspective, is 3rd June.

I counted seven potential candidates – which rapidly decreased to five, as the former Byrds and T-Rex drummers Michael Clarke and Mickey Finn had passed away in 1993 and 2003 respectively. However, amazingly, there was one person who fulfilled both criteria, and that lady was Anita Harris, who reached number 6 in the charts back in 1967 with a song called 'Just Loving You'.

Anita was scheduled to top the bill in a variety show being held at Darlington Civic Theatre. We bought tickets (front row, no less) and, on the appointed day, we made the short journey across the A66 in the hope of not only enjoying an afternoon's entertainment, but also meeting someone whose performances on television I can remember from way back when I was far younger and slimmer than I was in April 2016.

We arrived in my father's home town early enough to have a relaxing cup of coffee (or hot chocolate, in my case), and we wanted to have a scone each, but the woman in front of me ordered the second-to-last one. At least there was still one left; it was just a shame that Elaine had to miss out ...

That's a lie (of course): I had a raspberry and white chocolate muffin.

Onward to the theatre, and as the foyer began to fill, it became clear very quickly that this was one of those rare occasions when

Elaine and I would bring down the average age of the audience – quite considerably, in fact. Proceedings eventually got underway shortly after two o'clock, and I'd have to admit the show itself was actually a lot of fun.

Anita still had a wonderful voice, but there was a love for the songs and an emotion in her performance that absolutely radiated from the stage. Anita has had such an extraordinary career. She's played all the great venues and rubbed shoulders with so many of the biggest names in entertainment, yet on a Wednesday afternoon in Darlington, she was still able to reach out to every member of the audience and make them feel special – that is a gift.

As well as sounding great, Anita certainly looked fabulous from seat A9, but when I had the chance to actually meet her afterwards, I think it would be reasonable to say that she was a stunningly beautiful woman (she was 74 at the time). She was so charming to me and Elaine – we both got a hug – and although Anita was more than happy to have her picture taken, I was the only person with whom she actually posed for a photo.

As a postscript, in case you were wondering, the other four people to have had top 10 singles and share a birthday with Anita and yours truly are: Ian Hunter (Mott the Hoople), Deniece Williams, Suzi Quatro, and Kelly Jones of the Stereophonics.

You weren't wondering, were you?

There's really only one way to go after you've ventured into the top 10 ...

MEET SOMEONE WHO HAS
HAD A NUMBER ONE SINGLE

I think it's fair to say that the majority of chart-topping popstars don't exactly fall over themselves to perform in Teesside. Thankfully, in the autumn of 2017, three members of a band who had recorded three number ones during 1981 and 1982 appeared in Billingham. Elaine and I were in the third row of an expectant and worryingly over-excited audience at The Forum, awaiting the arrival onstage of Cheryl Baker, Jay Aston and Mike Nolan (formerly of Bucks Fizz – only now, complete with Bobby McVay, they were known simply as The Fizz).

The band won the Eurovision Song Contest with 'Making Your Mind Up' in April 1981, just four months before Blitz released their *All Out Attack* EP, the record that would make a massive and lasting impact on my life. I must admit I did wonder quite what my punk-loving teenage self would have made of the whole evening!

The 2017 line-up performed songs from past and present (a new album having been released a few weeks earlier), as well as a medley of 1980s hits and some enjoyable interaction with the audience. There was a particularly touching moment when Mike Nolan introduced the nurse who had looked after him during his six-week stay in hospital, following the 1984 coach crash in Newcastle that had so nearly claimed his life.

I went to the show with no real expectations, but I must be honest and say that The Fizz were great. The passage of time certainly hasn't dampened their enthusiasm, nor their ability to entertain. The highlight was undoubtedly 'Now Those Days Are Gone' with Nolan on lead vocals. The song was performed part a cappella; it was actually quite moving, and it was no surprise that a standing ovation followed.

But, of course, the main reason for making the short trip to Billingham was to meet any of the three original members of Bucks Fizz. There was a first-come first-served "meet and greet" after the show. I had asked how much it would cost; the answer was £20.

Quite expensive ...

Each!

Bloody expensive.

When the moment came, we were ushered forward to meet the quartet, who were sitting at a table positioned just outside the bar.

I managed to explain my reason for coming to see them. They all seemed really nice, and I received a genuinely positive reaction, especially from Cheryl and Mike. After a couple of minutes though, their "minder" said it was time for the photo. Elaine and I crouched behind the band (who remained seated) and basically it was *click, click, goodbye*!

It was lovely to spend even such a short time with people who had achieved so much in the music industry, but even though I now had photographic proof of the completion of my 93rd challenge, I also had an empty wallet ... and I could have murdered a takeaway.

MEET A PREMIER LEAGUE FOOTBALLER

I came up with the challenge of meeting a player from the game's top flight before my local club, Middlesbrough FC, got promoted. But their success offered me an opportunity of fulfilling the task without having to travel too far.

Yvonne Ferguson, from the football club, had already supported my project once before – by donating a signed shirt for auction back in 2014. She messaged me during the autumn of 2016 to say that she'd made an appointment for me to visit the club's training complex and meet a member of the first team squad.

Middlesbrough's training facilities are situated in the grounds of the equally attractive and imposing Rockcliffe Hall in Hurworth-on-Tees, just a few miles outside Darlington. I parked in the main car park – not another 08 reg in sight – and strolled into the impressive-looking training complex. After a short wait, I was met by Gordon Cox, and we had a thoroughly enjoyable chat about football past and present, as well as a bit of background to my challenges. He asked if there were any players I particularly wanted to meet. There were: George Friend and Ben Gibson.

There were several reasons for wanting to meet George and Ben. One was that we shared a mutual friend, and another was that I knew I would actually recognise both of them. A number of the squad had already passed by and I am rather embarrassed to admit that I simply did not know who some of them were. Had it been York City's 1983 / 84 Fourth Division squad, or any of Gateshead's Vauxhall Conference players from the mid-90s, it would have been no problem. But spotting someone who earned as much in a week as I did in a year proved a whole lot harder!

Anyway, just after George appeared, Ben arrived as well, and we spent 10 minutes or so talking about my reasons for being there, some of the challenges I had already undertaken, and what was planned for the future.

They asked me about dysthymia, how it affected my everyday life, and particularly how it impacted on my ability to take on some of the more daunting challenges, before we chatted about the pressures of playing top-level sport. Given the fact we had never met before and they were elite athletes playing in one of the best leagues in the world, I was really impressed by Ben and George.

I really appreciated the time they spent chatting to me when they were clearly busy, and the interest they showed in the whole subject of mental health.

MEET AN OLD SCHOOL FRIEND
FOR THE FIRST TIME IN 30 YEARS

I must admit that until the advent of social media, I was in contact with absolutely no one from my schooldays or brief foray into further education. That situation has now changed to a certain extent, and it's nice to occasionally share a memory or two with someone who knew me when I only had one chin.

When I was forced to look for work back in 2014, I registered on a business-related social networking site in the faint hope that fortune might flash a smile in my direction. Curiosity also got the better of me, and I took the opportunity to search for some names of former school classmates to see what they had done with their lives. And, more importantly, to see how many chins they'd acquired.

The people I found had all done well for themselves. I suppose that success was probably a pre-requisite for registering on the site in the first place. I did feel like the odd one out for a while – just as I had when I was at school. Back in those days, fees to attend what was a private school were waived in respect of sons of teachers (girls joined the sixth form for the first time in the late 1970s). By definition, then, all the other pupils came from families whose financial situation presumably ranged from comfortably off to loaded. Their backgrounds and lives were very different to mine, and in hindsight, it's no real surprise that there were certain people to whom I felt unable to relate. Evoking, albeit unintentionally, those long-suppressed feelings was a mistake (my fault for looking), and, as soon as I managed to get another job, I deleted my account.

During that time, though, I was contacted by Andrew Powles, who was a contemporary at St Peter's, one of the few people with whom I socialised outside school. I most definitely classed him as a friend. It was really good to hear from him and we began to exchange emails and keep up-to-date with each other's news. When Andrew brought his family to Harrogate for a short break during the Easter holidays, it was an ideal opportunity for me to make the short journey down to see him.

Meeting Andrew was different to almost all of the other tasks I'd completed up to that point. I had spent so much time planning and ticking specific tasks off the list, but this time the task was purely incidental.

Having the chance to catch up with an old friend I hadn't seen for something like 35 years was what mattered.

As I related earlier in the chapter, even the closest of friends essentially become strangers over time. But thankfully, when lives briefly converge, even fading memories of similar or shared experiences can compensate for the intervening years – and so it proved when I met Andrew. Of course, it was slightly surreal when he appeared. I recognised him, but when he spoke I realised I had no recollection of what his voice sounded like.

The conversation flowed effortlessly (or at least that was how it felt). Two hours passed quickly and from my perspective at least it was a hugely enjoyable evening. Andrew messaged me the following day to say pretty much the same and, for once, the tick that followed felt almost totally irrelevant.

CHAPTER 12

STEREOTYPES AND SELF-STIGMA

I grew up in an age when mental health was generally poorly understood and rarely discussed. I certainly have no clear recollection of the subject ever being raised at home or at school, but I also think it's fair to say I "understood" that it was a man's place to be strong and deal with life's trials and tribulations without showing any outward sign of weakness. It was never specifically stated; in those days, it was "just the way it was".

As I've said before, my mum and dad were both born shortly before the Second World War, so their own parents will have endured periods of almost unimaginable fear and hardship. Even if the stoic "stiff upper lip" was partially a show of defiance in those darkest of times, virtually every family will have been affected to some extent. And I can certainly appreciate how the collective strength that helped to rebuild our country would remain an expected aspect of everyday life into the 1950s and beyond.

I went to an all-boys school which held strict and traditional values. I called my dad "Sir" when I saw him during the day, I stood when an adult entered the room, and I always deferred to a woman (holding doors open, giving up seats, etc.). To this day I always hold a door open and let a lady pass first. Maybe it's no longer the politically correct thing to do ... but I was raised to show respect to a lady, and still believe it's important.

Throughout my childhood and into my teens, I can't recall ever seeing Dad get upset. When my episodes of intense sadness began, I found it impossible to understand how the man I looked up to was so strong, and yet I was so weak. In my own mind, I was letting my parents down. I was failing as a son ...

What I experienced was self-stigma, brought on by stereotypes about how a man should behave and what he should understand. And that's why I tried so very hard to keep those emotions hidden.

I didn't speak to anyone about how I felt. To be honest, I'm not sure who I could have turned to anyway, or what I would have said.

Things started to change when I went to Newcastle Polytechnic in the autumn of 1982. It took me quite a while to settle in and make friends, but over the months that followed, I found that I was really comfortable in female company.

People will have their own perception of my personality, but I'm naturally quite shy and very much an introvert. My sensitive side is much harder to keep hidden, but I've been lucky enough over the years to find a few really good friends with whom I can share my innermost thoughts and feelings. I also realised I had an ability to listen and empathise, which gave a real and lasting significance to the trust on which those friendships were built.

Thankfully, on most of the occasions when I've most needed to reach out, I have been able to spend time with someone I trusted. It did, however, take me far too long to recognise that the need to reach out was actually a symptom of my mental health condition.

I have learnt that dysthymia makes the concept of reaching out incredibly compelling. When you're at your lowest, it can make feel you so desperate to offload that someone who isn't a particularly good friend can suddenly (and inexplicably) become a person in whom you would willingly confide.

Looking at it with a clear head, it's obvious that it's a ridiculous (and actually quite selfish) notion. That level of trust can't just appear out of thin air, but if you show any hint of vulnerability, mental illness knows exactly how to take advantage.

You can't see it at the time, but talking to someone just because they happen to be there can make you feel incredibly guilty, once the initial relief of offloading wears off. But *not* talking simply allows dysthymia to strengthen its grip. It's hardly surprising that a downward spiral gathers pace when both outcomes to a certain situation are negative ...

Although I have had male friends who I would definitely say I trusted, I was 40 years old when the subject of mental health was first openly discussed around men – and even then I found it so hard to say the words. Speaking about my mental health experiences is now a massively important part of my life, but why did it take me so long to feel able to have that first "man-to-man" conversation?

Was I subconsciously worried how even a close mate would react?

Is it a generational thing?

And if I was a teenager now, would I have greater self-awareness and enough emotional strength to talk to someone, irrespective of their gender?

I do believe that aspects of my personality have been hugely influenced by the time and environment in which I grew up. That being the case, and given the fact that mental health has moved nearer the forefront of public consciousness – and masses of information is so easily available thanks to the wonders of technology – then I believe the respective answers to the last three questions would be: 'Yes, possibly', 'Yes, partly', and 'Yes, definitely.'

I honestly think that if I was a teenager now, in the digital age, stereotyping and self-stigma would have far less of a grip on me.

The idea that I avoided talking to certain people just in case they reacted unfavourably seems a bit unfair now. How they would respond to a difficult subject wasn't my judgement to make. If I'd trusted someone enough to think I could open up to them in the first place, then their gender should have been irrelevant.

And yet the first time the opportunity to talk to a man about my issues presented itself, I hesitated.

Perhaps there was a barrier, some subconscious sense of shame or embarrassment that I wasn't immediately able to overcome. Maybe I found it so difficult simply because I hadn't opened up to a male friend before.

Or has the subsequent passage of time made the answer to these questions largely irrelevant?

As is happens, whether I could, would or should have been able to talk freely in male company doesn't really matter now. What is more significant is that I was lucky enough to have a small number of female friends with whom I was able to share thoughts and feelings.

Years ago, some would have called me soft or weak for not being able to deal with my emotions (there was certainly a time when that's how I saw myself). Yet, almost four decades later, I'm apparently strong and brave for speaking out about my condition!

Who knew?

I've changed so much (and so quickly) as my self-awareness has increased, and now I have no issue talking or listening to *anyone* on the subject of mental health. I suppose it's slightly disappointing that it took me so long to get to this point (better late than never), but that only increases my admiration for all the young people who speak so openly, knowledgeably and often passionately about the most difficult aspects of mental illness.

Much as I have tried to show that it absolutely is okay to talk and to ask for help, I firmly believe that the younger generation holds the key to how mental health conditions are discussed, detected, treated and managed. Time will tell, but from what I have seen and heard, it looks like the future is in caring hands.

CHAPTER 13

TO DARE IS TO DO

HAVE A BELATED FIRST GO
ON A ROLLERCOASTER

Along with my friend Nik and sisters Steph and Jeni from work, I set off for the 2014 Hoppings fair on Newcastle's Town Moor – not only for my rollercoaster debut, but also for my first ever visit to an annual fair whose arrival apparently always provokes a monsoon. Among the seemingly never-ending array of rides and stalls was The Wild Mouse, part rollercoaster, part (as I was soon to discover) Waltzer. I was slightly surprised that the ride took its name from a cute little furry rodent. If you were going to go down the animal route, wouldn't you have chosen something bigger, something with a bit of a presence?

Actually, perhaps the mouse reference had something to do with the regular squeaking sounds that could be heard during the ride's warm-up run ...

Not a great sign, but undeterred I paid my £3 and took my seat. A padded metal bar was raised up over my lap. It didn't feel very stable – and I didn't feel very safe.

The "roller" bit soon got underway, and any prospect of fun disappeared when the first 90-degree turn was followed by a fairly rapid descent (which I presume was the "coaster" part). I genuinely thought I was going to be thrown from my seat, and spent the rest of the ride clinging on to the safety bar for dear life, with Nik and Steph's laughter and screams ringing in my good ear.

If I'd kept my eyes open, I might have spotted the next right-angled turn, but I would never have been prepared for my seat starting to spin round and round at the same bloody time. Had I eaten a substantial dinner, this was the moment when it would have been projected far and wide across the Town Moor, but thankfully the contents of my stomach remained in their proper place until the ordeal ... sorry, the *ride* ... was over.

The girls were fine, but I was decidedly dizzy and struggling to walk in a straight line. I suppose the whole idea of a challenge is that it's not supposed to be easy, and not necessarily fun either. Just as well, because this was neither – and I made a very serious mental note to self never to try anything even remotely fairground related ever again.

ATTEMPT THE HOTTEST CURRY ON THE MENU

In the autumn of 2014, Elaine and I ventured into Jamal's Indian restaurant, a recommended establishment close to Middlesbrough town centre. After a quick chat with the owner, I ordered the dish that would guarantee completion of the challenge.

The meal in question was called Chicken Kalia, apparently a traditional Mauritian recipe, which was then spiced according to individual preference. I thought the sauce would be hot enough to kill off any taste, but that wasn't the case at all. The curry had a lovely aromatic flavour – hardly a challenge at all.

I paused just for a moment to ask Elaine if she was enjoying her Rogan Josh, and that was all the time it took for my mouth to suddenly feel like it was on fire. It was like I'd swallowed a furnace. My lips started tingling and it took several gulps of water before the sensation started to wear off.

Obviously I finished the whole meal (I'm no quitter in the curry department). I also finished what was left of the jug of water (much to Elaine's amusement), and as soon as I'd recovered the power of speech I asked the owner about the recipe. The heat was courtesy of the presence of the naga chilli among the ingredients. Chilli strength is calculated using something called the Scovill scale, named after its creator Wilbur Scovill in 1912. Apparently the naga chilli is one of the hottest varieties and has been measured at over one million on the Scovill scale, although as far as assessing the potency or otherwise of spicy food is concerned, I have my own foolproof post-meal method.

I had also read that the naga chilli would sometimes be smeared onto fences, or somehow used as part of a smoke bomb, to ward off wild elephants. I wasn't entirely sure whether or not those ideas were effective in north eastern India, but the lack of elephants on Corporation Road suggested they worked fine over here.

GET A TATTOO

This personal challenge meant a lot to me as it made a permanent difference to my physical appearance.

The reason I added getting a tattoo to the list was to demonstrate just how seriously I was taking the whole challenge. It highlighted the importance I placed in the cause for which I was raising funds during those initial 12 months.

So many of the tasks were a sort of "moment in time", a meeting or an event that passed with little more than a photographic record for posterity, but this was totally different. My body now bears a constant reminder of the whole adventure – and also of the person who changed my life.

No turning back!

Ste Carne, who ran a local tattoo parlour, was kind enough to agree to carry out the work – even more generous was his offer to donate the cost of the tattoo to my fundraising page. Strangely, as someone for whom a rollercoaster ride had proved genuinely terrifying, I wasn't nervous at all about visiting Ste's studio. A small design had been prepared, and was duly transferred onto the top of my back, just under my right shoulder, after my manly hairs had been removed.

I chose that side because I'm left-handed. You know, just in case something went badly wrong and my right arm fell off ...

Ste chatted through everything, and made sure I was totally comfortable before getting underway. I was expecting it to hurt a bit, and although I could obviously feel the needle, it certainly wasn't painful. As a blood donor, I had given 28 pints of Kirby "gold top", so I was well aware of the effect that a needle could have on some people. Ste certainly had one or two tales of his own to tell ...

After the outline was completed, there was a change of needle to fill in the design, and then back to the first needle to finish off. And that was it; probably no more than 20 minutes.

So, what did I get done?

The initials "R" (for me) and "E" (for Elaine) in old English lettering. I know I should have put Elaine's initial first, but then it would have looked like I'd got a tattoo commemorating the Queen!

Incidentally, the 100th and final challenge was also tattoo related. The design was a semicolon, the punctuation mark widely adopted as a symbol of mental health awareness, preceded by the number 100 (to represent the number of metres I finished behind Chris Cook in our 100-metre swimming race). The tattoo now adorns the left side of my chest, right where the pectoralis major muscle would be ... if I had one.

GO TOPLESS ON SOCIAL MEDIA

During the late summer of 2014, I made a concerted effort to lose some weight. By the end of the first week in August I'd managed to shed a stone, and decided the time was as right as it was ever going to be to take on what was actually more of a dare than a challenge:

To go topless on social media. A ridiculous idea, but the cause was more important than my feelings.

Actually, it wasn't, but I think it looks quite good on paper.

Armed with my trusty camera, and minus the excess poundage, I took the photo, uploaded it, and moved on with my life ...

Clearly, I would like to have said the picture posted of my muscular torso was the first one I took – just point, press and job done. But I would be lying.

I wasn't counting (to be honest, I'd lost count), but the selfie that went public was probably in the region of the 200th attempt. One or two weren't too bad, but the majority were awful. And it said a lot that the second-best shot was one when I was fiddling with the settings on the back of the camera and pressed the shutter by accident.

It was of the fireplace.

ALLOW SARAH FROM WORK
TO DYE MY HAIR PINK

The chapter ends with something that was probably midway between a suggestion and a dare, given to me by Sarah Stringer, a colleague from work.

I received plenty of challenge ideas over the four years, most of which were discarded due to the likelihood of very serious injury, but I included this one not because I particularly wanted someone to turn what hair I had left some luminous pink colour, but because of how much Sarah had achieved during the time I had known her.

She had not only transformed herself from someone who rarely exercised to an athlete capable of running a marathon inside four hours, but she also devoted a lot of free time to a Northallerton-based group, which helped people to get back into running and enjoy the physical and mental health benefits of regular exercise. It felt like a fitting link to my mental health campaigning.

Sarah was the inspiration behind the desire to complete a marathon of my own – mine would be on a rowing machine –

and agreeing to let Sarah dye my hair was, in a sense, a way of quietly appreciating everything she had accomplished.

The challenge was added to the list at the start of 2017; it seemed a good idea at the time. But as dye-day drew ever nearer, I began to seriously question my judgement. I started to search the internet for quick tips for removing the semi-permanent concoction that was to be smeared over my hair – or head, for those barren areas.

I was 53. Honestly, what was I thinking?!

Sarah's "salon" was actually the kitchen at work, and it wasn't exactly designed for any hair-related activity. That said, the application of the dye was curiously therapeutic, and I felt fairly relaxed during the subsequent half-hour I had to sit while the transformation took place.

As Sarah washed off the dye mixture and towel-dried my hair, I was all too aware of the chuckles and occasional gasps from those popping into the kitchen. It quickly became clear that my hair wasn't pastel pink, it was shocking pink … a fact confirmed by the first of a number of photos that I was shown.

I looked ridiculous, but do you know what? I didn't care.

Several people had said I should have dyed my eyebrows or facial hair as well … but all I'd done was accepted the "challenge" I'd been given. Part of me was (rightly or wrongly) actually irritated that others wanted me to take things one step further. Wasn't it enough to be seen in public with bright pink hair?

I wasn't bothered in the slightest about being stared at, or even laughed at. But equally, I wanted people to know *why* my hair had been coloured. It definitely wasn't a fashion statement, so there had to be another reason …

What I found really interesting was the notion that I could have gone through some sort of routine (something as simple as going for a walk perhaps) day after day, month after month, year after year, and barely been noticed. Certainly no one would have guessed I had a mental health condition. Yet something as arguably irrelevant as hair colour could suddenly make you visible; and how many people would then form a lasting "first impression" of someone they'd unknowingly passed any number of times before?

How many other people are ignored or overlooked as they go about their daily business ... people who could be struggling to cope with an illness or condition that no one can see? Well, the statistics say it's every fourth person – completely irrespective of hair colour or appearance. Maybe that's something worth just bearing in mind when you're walking along a busy high street.

CHAPTER 14

WALK A MILE IN ANOTHER'S SHOES

VISIT A MOSQUE

I first encountered Imran Naeem and Zakir "Zak" Mahmoud through work back in 2013, and they have since become great friends and supporters of my challenges. After our first meeting I really wanted to learn more about their Muslim faith, so as soon as the opportunity arose, we went for a coffee and a chat.

From a religious (and arguably philosophical) standpoint, I have always been seated very comfortably astride the proverbial fence. I was raised within the Church of England, but class myself as agnostic. I apparently lean towards theism – who knew?! I certainly don't disbelieve in the concept of God. I simply don't know if He exists.

But the beliefs I do have are borne from personal experience and I am perfectly comfortable with my feelings towards religion in general. I'm also more than capable of respecting those who have a faith, but having worked alongside some of the Muslim community, and given the general media profile of Islam, I wanted to delve beneath the newspaper articles and find out a little bit more.

For those Muslims in the North East who spend time within their extended communities, trying to challenge stereotypes and break down barriers is incredibly difficult. But seeing the human reaction to various truly shocking events (I sat down with Imran and Zak just over six months after the brutal murder of Lee Rigby) and hearing how *12 months* of hard and positive work could be undone in one horrific moment – well, it certainly made me stop and think.

The three of us chatted through things as diverse as the origins of the universe and the Sixth Pillar of Faith, as well as *Star Wars* and *Doctor Who*! I found the part of the conversation about the Sixth Pillar absolutely fascinating. That final pillar relates to fate, or divine predestination – Imran and Zak called it the "Decree". Essentially (and I think I've got this right) for some Muslims, it relates to the ability for free will to still exist in lives and a world where all events are pre-determined and known to Allah. Take religion out of the equation and you basically have the concept of compatibilism.

The parallel between my own ideals and a religion about which I know very little was a real surprise.

At no point was I made to feel uncomfortable for my lack of understanding (despite being so far out of my depth) and my own points of view were totally respected. I left with the same beliefs I'd had when I arrived, but with a small, yet real insight into the faith that guides the lives of so many people.

That meeting led directly to one of my 2014 challenges, as Imran invited me to come along for Friday prayers at the Dar ul Islam Central Mosque in Middlesbrough. I must admit I felt slightly nervous beforehand. It was to be a completely new experience and, rightly or wrongly, I saw myself very much as the odd man out.

Anyway, with shoes safely removed, I sat at the back of the room, which filled steadily as the clock ticked towards half past twelve. On arrival there was time for quiet individual prayer, the precise form of which seemed to vary. But it was apparent that there was a significant number of different cultural backgrounds or countries of origin represented, all brought together by a shared faith.

The Imam gave a sermon, the majority of which was in English – which helped! I'm sure his words resonated strongly with the majority of those in the room, but I just listened intently and was certainly interested by what he had to say.

Due entirely to media stereotyping, I had expected the sermon to be delivered forcefully, perhaps even aggressively. But that absolutely wasn't the case. There were definite parallels with the style of delivery I would have heard in Church of England services when I was much younger, and there was something almost pleasing about having my preconceptions proved wrong.

I should also add that I got pins and needles in my right foot, and a particularly hot back caused by the pipe against which I was resting. But I stayed admirably still throughout!

After the sermon, there were more regimented prayers (in Arabic), and I was struck by the contrast between the initial individual prayer and reflection and the final group prayers, which clearly united those in attendance. I was also acutely aware that I was the only person sitting down among the rows of standing men.

That feeling of self-consciousness increased sharply when everyone knelt down and my head suddenly appeared over the top!

Thankfully everyone stood up. Phew!

Then knelt down again. Drat!

With prayer over, the room started to empty. But before he left, the Imam came over and greeted me with a traditional hug, which I certainly hadn't expected. I thanked him for allowing me to come into the Mosque and listen to his sermon, and was duly invited to return in the future.

Shattered preconception number two: a non-Muslim being so warmly welcomed by someone of such standing. It was becoming clear that there were many members of the local Islamic community who appreciated when genuine interest was shown in their culture and beliefs – and that open, non-judgemental conversations could take place with non-Muslims. Mutual respect *and* friendship could grow out of outward diversity …

The world we live in now is so far removed from the one in which I grew up. I don't really know if there were many people from black or minority ethnic backgrounds living in York during the late 1960s and early 1970s, but I certainly can't remember seeing any. Nowadays though, this country is home to such an amazing mix of cultures and communities and my opinion (which I accept is simplistic) is that I have two choices:

Try to spend time with people whose life experiences are in whatever way, and to whatever extent, different to mine …

Or don't.

And it's absolutely not restricted to religion … take the whole subject of mental health, for example. Talk, ask questions, learn, understand, share and hopefully enrich each other's lives.

OBSERVE RAMADAN FOR A DAY AND SHARE REFLECTIONS WITH MY MUSLIM FRIENDS

In both 2014 and 2015, I decided to fast out of respect for Imran, Zak and the rest of the Muslim community during the month of Ramadan (not the month, I hasten to add, but rather for just one day). No food or water from first light through to sunset, the exact timing of which was always going to be an issue given how little evening sun we'd actually seen over recent summers.

I plumped for 9.50pm.

In 2014, my first mistake was waking up at 5.00am to find the sun was already shining and it was therefore too late to drink copious amounts of water and stuff my face with pretty much anything I could lay my hands on. Bit of a schoolboy error, as I would basically have to go 24 hours without food. The Ramadan fast extends to drinking as well, although there are a few exceptions, one of which is travelling. As I had to drive the 100-mile round trip to Newcastle, I did allow myself a couple of gulps of water on the way home, to ensure that if my body suffered any adverse reaction, it wouldn't be while I was doing 70mph down the A19.

Those two sips aside, I essentially went a full day without food or drink. There were some difficult moments – about 23.5 out of the 24 hours, really.

Actually, after about two o'clock, I was fine. The lunch period was definitely the worst time, as my colleagues devoured their various meals and snacks. It was more the smell of the food than watching them eat that caused me serious discomfort ... but I watched them nonetheless.

Once I got home and the clock ticked past five ... six ... seven o'clock, I knew I was going to complete the fast – and in a way, I was quite proud of myself. Obviously, there was no comparison with those who do this for a month at a time. I don't think I could do that (I love cake too much), but given that my body is not conditioned to going without food – and I missed the opportunity of an early morning binge – I thought I'd done okay.

Fasting for a day during Ramadan was duly added to my list of 2015 challenges. I actually managed to complete two days (albeit not concurrently). Part of the whole theme behind my challenges was to get the people who were helping me to understand mental health, and so it felt right to try to understand others too. Respect was also part of the reason behind fasting and I used those two days as a time for reflection. I spent quiet moments remembering those who had helped shape the person I had become.

Four people who made a massive difference were my grandparents – on Dad's side, Gertie and Eric (Gran and Grandad), and on Mum's side they were Mary and Les (Nannie and Grandad). They have all long since passed away, but I often think about them.

One effect of fasting was that it really concentrated the mind, and whenever I felt hungry (which was most of the time), I tried to use memories of my grandparents as a positive distraction. I consider myself blessed to have spent so much time with four such wonderful people: Gran and Grandad in Darlington, and Nannie and Grandad in the small Leicestershire village of Croft.

It's strange, but even now I can clearly picture Nannie and Grandad's house just as it was all those years ago. I can smell the cigarettes and the toast made under the grill every morning. I can hear the noise of the overnight freight trains on the nearby railway line, the sound of Nannie and Grandad's voices ... and the seemingly constant laughter. I'm sure their lives weren't as simple as they appeared through innocent young eyes, but my grandparents each did whatever they could to make my childhood special. I just wish there was a way I could see them all one more time to tell them how much I love and miss them.

Towards the end of Ramadan, Elaine and I were invited to a Middlesbrough restaurant to attend an annual iftar (breaking of the fast) hosted by members of the Islamic Diversity Centre. This was the second year that we'd been invited to what was a fantastic opportunity for Muslims and non-Muslims to come together and enjoy company and conversation that effortlessly bridged cultural and religious differences.

Inside the restaurant, we caught up with a few friends and also had a chance to natter with a number of people we hadn't met before. There were a couple of talks about the meaning of Ramadan and the effects (and apparent benefits) of fasting. A couple of non-Muslims who had observed the fast were then invited to chat about their experiences, and every speaker had something interesting to say – until it was my turn.

One day I'll learn that if you're going to stand up with a microphone, it's best to have some idea about what you're going to say.

In the end I spoke about my great-great-grandmother Jane Kirby, who was another relative I had thought about during the two days I had fasted. Jane gave birth to her son (my great grandfather John) in a workhouse, and worked her fingers to the bone making matchboxes simply to survive. How she found the strength to keep going in such poverty I cannot possibly imagine, but the simple fact remains that I am only here because she did.

In my wallet, I have a coin. It is a half crown from 1879, the year John Kirby was born. Back then, half a crown was worth two shillings and sixpence (12½p post decimalisation). It might not seem much, but Jane would have had to work for *three weeks* to earn that one coin. In her lifetime, Jane may have been the lowest of the low in terms of social class. And yet to me she was, and will always be, an inspiration.

When the time came to break the fast, I picked up what Zak had convinced me was a chocolate. I'd been so looking forward to that first mouthful ...

It was a date – the very definition of "disappointment"!

The fact I am not a Muslim has never been of any consequence to my friends within the community; they respect the values and beliefs that are important to me, just as I respect the faith that guides their lives.

SPEND AN EVENING WORKING IN A SOUP KITCHEN

There are members of the local community who do a lot of work to support those less fortunate than themselves – work that often goes unnoticed by the majority – and I really wanted to take part in an event to find out about the difference that they make to communities.

I was aware of a soup kitchen for the homeless, run through the One Ummah organisation (which provides aid to those in need around the world), and so I sent an email asking if I could volunteer for an evening. When the reply came, it was from someone I knew (which was a bit of a blow because I'd really exaggerated what a nice bloke I was) and arrangements were made for me to go along to Middlesbrough's International Community Centre one Saturday evening in August 2016.

Atif, Imran, Pav and Sab were already busy setting up the hall when I arrived – putting out tables and chairs, boiling the water in the urn for the hot drinks and putting the food (pizza and rice) into containers. At six o'clock it was time to welcome those who had come along for what is now a regular fortnightly chance to have a hot meal and a drink in comfortable surroundings. I didn't count the exact number, but there were probably around 40 people in the hall.

I helped Atif with making the teas and coffees. All these faces filed past, each with their own life, their own story. It was another of those moments that would later make me pause for contemplation. I didn't really know or understand enough to appreciate just how tough their individual situations might be, but I was touched by their gratitude for being given something that most of us would simply take for granted.

It wasn't pity. Seeing people in need both accepting – and appreciating – an offer of help gave me a positive feeling. Homelessness has its own stigma, as has mental health too, but just as there are some battling debilitating and unseen illness, others have to contend with different forms of hardship – often with quite humbling dignity.

That evening might have been another tick in the box as far as the challenges were concerned. But the reality was so much more important.

TAKE PART IN A LOCAL CHARITY EVENT

I have decided to add one further challenge to this particular chapter because of its direct connection with the homeless. On the evening of the second Friday in May 2017, Elaine and I took part in the Big Teesside Sleepout, an event organised by the Middlesbrough & Teesside Philanthropic Foundation to raise awareness of (and funds for) homelessness and poverty in the region.

It was going to be a new experience for both of us, so much so that we had to borrow a sleeping bag and purchase a couple of foam mats. The five-day weather forecast had predicted rain during the night, and sure enough Friday morning was cloudy and relatively cool following a glorious Wednesday and Thursday. However, as the day progressed, the temperature remained fairly mild, and the final forecast we heard suggested that the rain would linger in the west of the country.

We were set for a dry night – something of a relief.

We were advised to wear plenty of layers, so that's exactly what we did: we wore thermal vests, jumpers, hoodies and waterproof jackets just in case the forecaster had made a Michael Fish-style blunder. We put on hats, gloves and thermal socks for the old extremities and we were almost ready for the off.

There are actually two sleepouts every year – one in summer, the other towards the end of the year. The later event is apparently much more popular (or perhaps "well-attended" might be a more appropriate phrase), with often three or four times as many participants than the 30 or so that joined us at Middlesbrough College.

When we arrived, we had to sign a disclaimer that said something along the lines of: "You accept you may be injured or even die". I was fully prepared to go home with a sore back, but to be honest, I felt less inclined to perish in the attempt.

But no matter, we completed the form and set up our double sleeping bag and pillows in the designated area outside the main building.

Much as the event aimed to highlight the hardship faced by the homeless and the poor, we had the luxury of being given a warm meal (soup or jacket potato), hot drinks and access to toilet facilities. What we were about to experience was therefore only a taste of the reality faced by so many on a nightly basis, but I suppose it was important to actually ensure a decent attendance – and help to raise as much as possible towards supporting those most in need.

Thanks to the generosity of friends and family, we had raised £185. The total donated on the night exceeded £5,000, the news of which was a boost as we headed back outside.

I wasn't expecting to get too much sleep, but after a couple of poor nights during the week, I was certainly tired. I snuggled into the sleeping bag, gloves and hat on, but shoes off, closed my eyes and started to drift. There was a hum of conversation from those around us that was more relaxing than annoying, and I reckon I was probably asleep by half past ten.

Unsurprisingly, it wasn't easy to stay comfortable for long periods, and I stirred several times in order to readjust my position – and to remove my hat and gloves.

Would you believe I was too warm?!

I remember thinking each time I woke that, despite a couple of aches and a bit of cramp, this was okay for only one night. It wasn't even cold or wet.

How do people manage when this isn't just a one-off? If it started to rain ... when the temperature dropped ...

It feels so easy to take the lives we have for granted.

I woke properly at about five o'clock. The sun was starting to rise, and it was a beautiful morning. Elaine was still fast asleep, but she opened her eyes about half an hour later, having also had a far less difficult night than we'd probably both expected. The event (which was extremely well organised) ended at six o'clock, and people started to drift off back to their respective homes for the weekend. Within half an hour we were sitting in our living room ... and it was basically a normal (albeit early) start to what would hopefully be a normal day.

But this time we had a far greater appreciation of the fact that not everybody's "normal" was the same.

CHAPTER 15

AT THE DOUBLE

Given the incredible amount of support I've received from so many people throughout the duration of the challenges (viz. the long list of genuine thanks at the back of the book), it would seem unfair to single out any particular names – but that's what I'm going to do ...

This chapter is not intended to lessen the impact of anyone and everyone who has been kind enough to get involved, but it feels right to mention a couple of individuals whose help and participation extended into multiple tasks: Geraldine "Gel" Williams and Glen Durrant.

Ladies (or rather lady) first ...

PLAY GOAL SHOOTER IN A NETBALL TEAM

I first met Gel in 2014. She was (and is) the head coach at Grangetown Netball Club, runs a couple of pubs and bars in Normanby, and does an awful lot more work besides – almost always for the benefit of the local community. I honestly don't know how she manages to do so much, but thankfully she found the time to have a chat with me about my netball challenge. And you will soon see just how much has happened since that first meeting.

When she was a teenager, my younger daughter Rebecca played club and county netball – primarily as a goal shooter. I used to love going to watch her play, but time moves on, priorities change, and Becca now lives and works in Scotland. She has played a bit of netball since moving north of the border, but for her dad, taking part in a game of netball was to be a brand-new experience.

Gel had invited me down to Grangetown Youth & Community Centre to take part in a practice match towards the end of a training session (in August 2014). At the time, the senior side played in the second division of the National Premier League, and were ranked within the country's top 20 clubs. I was very much thrown in at the deep end, then!

But despite my chronic hip problem, I had actually done quite a lot to prepare for my "debut". I'd lost a stone in weight, been pedalling around 40 miles a week on the exercise bike – and I'd watched loads of netball from that summer's Glasgow Commonwealth Games.

What could possibly go wrong?

Well, I knew that at best I'd be struggling to walk the following morning, but I hoped that the old limbs would be able to keep me upright long enough to get me through another sporting challenge.

On the appointed evening, I turned up at Grangetown's Youth & Community Centre about an hour before the moment of truth. As I watched the girls being put through their paces, the nerves kicked in, and I started to question the wisdom of including this challenge in the list.

There was a whole world of difference between young and athletic, and old and immobile. Oh yes, and they were all excellent netball players, while I'd ... er ... watched a bit of the Commonwealth Games.

I spent a few minutes warming up in the corridor outside the sports hall. One thing I'd learnt from the challenges was how to smile for a photo. So I gave the security camera one of my best grins every time I skipped past. I might even have waved at one point – it just seemed the polite thing to do.

Some of the girls knew I was coming, but I accept it must have been an incongruous sight as I entered the main hall. I had a few practice shots at a basketball hoop at the side of the hall, before being handed the goal shooter bib. I strolled onto the court, the whistle went and just like that, we were underway.

I had to check the colour of my bib (blue) because I honestly wasn't sure who was on my side! I wasn't expecting to have too much trouble catching the ball, but getting in a position where it could be thrown to me was a different matter altogether. I was being "marked" by a young lady called Amy, who had this annoying habit of getting in the way in between me and the ball. It certainly didn't seem very sporting!

All I can remember when I first received the ball was someone yelling 'Shoot!' from the side lines. I didn't that time, but the attempts I had during the first half all missed. Most were close – one agonisingly so – but one shot missed by a margin that was big enough for it to be more accurately described as a pass.

My throat had dried up completely, but I was really enjoying myself. And even though I knew I was totally out of my depth, it was still fantastic to get that briefest flicker of memory of how it used to feel to play a competitive team sport. A couple more shooting chances came my way in the second half and finally I managed to project the ball into and through the hoop, rather than at it. I'd like to think the crowd went wild!

One more shrill blast on the whistle and it was all over. At the end of the session, the girls all posed for the obligatory photo. It was the easiest "spot the odd one out" competition in history.

TAKE TO THE NETBALL COURT FOR A SECOND (AND DEFINITELY FINAL) TIME

I'd had such a great time that I decided to come out of retirement and do it all again the following year. For a return that could only be described as the total opposite of eagerly anticipated, there were two major differences. Firstly, the venue was the very impressive Middlesbrough Sports Village, and secondly, my position had been changed to goalkeeper. When I arrived, the girls were just about to start a full practice match, so I settled down to watch – and, hopefully, learn – before taking my place at the heart of the defence alongside club captain Vicky Rees.

When I'd tried my hand as a shooter, I found that the ball was too big and the net way too small (and too high up). Evidently all that had changed during the intervening 12 months because shots were finding the target with almost ridiculous regularity.

At least I'd had the decency to make the game look difficult!

Within a minute of the game starting, I managed to collide with the post. In my defence, I was trying to track my shooter – I failed. It hurt.

It was great to witness at first-hand the pace at which the game is played, the quality of movement, awareness, and the athleticism of everyone on court – with one elderly, portly exception. I did wear Grangetown colours in an attempt to look the part, and even managed to make a couple of interceptions (more by luck than judgement, I hasten to add). But if I was to summarise my performance in one word, it would be "clumsy" – although one other adjective beginning with "c" was also rather apt.

In between my two netball outings, I completed what would be the first of two 12-hour solo darts marathons at The Cleveland Inn, a pub that just happened to be managed by ... Gel.

Gel and Glen – I can't thank them enough.

COMPLETE A 12-HOUR SOLO DARTS MARATHON

The event took place between 8.00am and 8.00pm on 16th May 2015. BBC Radio Tees agreed to come along and do a live interview just before I got started, and Glen Durrant had offered to drop in at lunchtime and play a few legs en route to the Welsh Open. Members of the Grangetown squad would be popping in at various points during the day; there was a buffet, a raffle – and 12 hours of me trying to hit a decent score or two.

I practised religiously (every Sunday), and in the April I had the chance to test my progress with a leg of 701 against Scott "Scotty Dog" Mitchell, who at the time was the incumbent BDO World Champion. Elaine and I had the pleasure of sitting with Glen and Scott at the exhibition, which was held in Great Ayton; it was fascinating to chat to Scott about his recent Lakeside triumph and to try to understand a little about what goes through the mind of someone who has, in his hand, a dart that will change his life forever – but only if it lands in the 8mm width of the right double.

I have so much admiration for Scott, Glen and those other top players whose physical and mental self-control is strong enough for them to produce the same levels of performance under extreme pressure as they do away from the bright lights and cameras. And for Scott Mitchell, if hitting that winning double top and lifting the trophy didn't make him appreciate the scale of his wonderful achievements, then surely having the wonderfully named Piddle Brewery produce a beer in his honour must have been the moment of ultimate realisation!

It was Scott's opening game of the evening, so he was not (thankfully) at his best, but I threw well, managed to stay in touch and thanks to a (fanfare, drum roll, etc.) throw of 140, was actually first to finish. On 85, I wasn't good enough to get a shot at a double or the bull, and with that the chance was gone, as Scott stepped up and hit the winning double six. No disappointment though – I'd given the world champion a half-decent game, and recorded that elusive ton-plus score in the process. It was the perfect boost of confidence in the lead up to the marathon.

Come the day, I arrived at the pub just after 7.30am to get everything ready and have a few throws at the board. The reporter from BBC Radio Tees arrived, and we had a brief chat about what I was going to be asked during the brief live segment that was to follow. On the stroke of eight o'clock, proceedings were officially underway – and incredibly, the first three darts ended in the treble 20!

The subsequent radio interview went well, although in fairness darts doesn't really lend itself to an audio format. Make three thudding noises and just make up a decent score – no one would ever know. After that, it was very much a case of getting through the day an hour at a time. People came, people went; there were good scores and crap scores. Glen turned up, gave me a darting lesson and then headed off to Wales (where he won the Welsh Open and became BDO World Number One in the process). More people came and went; a few stayed. My back seized up … badly.

But by eight o'clock in the evening, I projected the final three darts at the board, and the marathon was over. I managed four maximums and 292 other scores of one hundred or more … and I had one black big toenail, the pain from which was partially numbed when Gel brought through a tray of tequila shots – my first bit of alcohol of the day.

The marathon raised £500 for the netball club. It was (in its own way) an enjoyable day, although, as expected, I couldn't walk the following morning.

Just for the record, the following year's event resulted in no fewer than seven majestic throws of 180, another whitewash at the hands of Glen Durrant, and a lovely surprise visit from my local MP Anna Turley. Oh, and another black big toenail.

PUT MY OLD, ACHING BODY
THROUGH A YOGA SESSION

For this challenge I was put through my paces (in both yoga and also Pilates) by Grangetown captain Vicky Rees, who runs Studio 21 on Yarm High Street.

Vicky and I had known each other for quite a while, but I was still nervous at the prospect of what would be a totally new experience. To say my body is a wreck would be a bit of an understatement, and I was genuinely concerned that my hips, back or pretty much any other part of me wouldn't make it through the session.

The other reason for my trepidation was that the last time Vicky had been part of one of my challenges it was allegedly as a "teammate" in my second netball performance. Despite being on the same side, there is a photo of Vicky jogging past me during the game with a huge grin on her face – caused, no doubt, by another failed attempted interception.

And if she thought my efforts on the netball court were funny ...

In fairness, I needn't have worried. Vicky had prepared a plan for me in advance, but before getting underway, I had to complete a health questionnaire. We then discussed the highlighted areas of concern (of which there were many) and, throughout the hour, Vicky was always able to adapt aspects of the positions and exercises to suit my own mobility. She began with work on my posture and some basic yoga stretches, before a series of exercises on the Pilates reformer, and some breathing techniques to finish.

Everything was fully explained and demonstrated – and I left with a couple of exercises to practise that might hopefully help with my lifelong round-shouldered posture. I found the stretching quite difficult and surprisingly tiring. I won't deny that it was hard work.

Thankfully Vicky was fantastic; she kept a close eye on how I was doing, gave me plenty of advice, and made sure everything was done at a pace and level to suit me.

The Pilates reformer looked like an ancient instrument of torture, but I actually quite enjoyed the various exercises. Although, there was a slight moment of panic when Vicky heard a "grating" noise in my ankle when I did the Achilles tendon stretch ...

Fetch that health questionnaire!

Just for the record, Pilates was invented by a German named Joseph Pilates – whereas I believe yoga was created by a smarter than average inhabitant of Jellystone Park.

HAVE A GAME OF 501 AGAINST AN INTERNATIONAL DARTS PLAYER

One of the best things about this whole adventure has been the friendships that have grown from an initial request for help. One such friendship developed from an email asking for a game of darts, and while I spent the next four years attempting various different things, the person in question became a world champion.

I added darts to the original list of challenges because after being a reasonable player in my teens, I began to suffer from what is known as "dartitis". Effectively, this is a nervous condition that, in my case, prevented me from even letting go of a dart, let alone throwing it remotely accurately. Rather than expose myself to even the possibility of humiliation, I stopped playing in public. I did occasionally have a game on my own in the garage (the board was later transferred to the conservatory, by which time I'd become quite proficient at playing in sub-zero temperatures), but until I arranged to meet Glen Durrant, I basically hadn't played darts against an opponent for something approaching a quarter of a century.

Glen only lived a couple of miles away, and we met at the North Ormesby Working Men's Club. Unsurprisingly, I was nervous when I met Glen, but he chatted away and really helped me relax (well, a bit). That said, I think we were both surprised when my first three darts landed not only in the board, but in the 20. There were plenty of wayward arrows over the next 10 or 15 minutes, but more than a few landed near where I was aiming, and so we decided it was about time to set the electronic scorer to 501 and play a proper game.

It was brilliant to stand behind Glen and watch as he hit big score after big score. I hit a ton in the second game and a few more in the legs that followed. I even managed one 140, with the third dart very close indeed to finding the treble for a most unlikely maximum. In the second-to-last game, I threw my most consistent darts and actually had two shots at a double to sneak the leg. I missed, though.

But while the competitor in me was annoyed, I was only too aware that in years gone by I would have just stood there at the oche, with a trembling left arm and precious little chance of letting the dart go – so this had actually been a real achievement.

Glen closed out the last game with a brilliant 149 finish – just as I was finding my range – he was clearly a top-class player, but he was also incredibly encouraging throughout.

During the evening, he offered me the chance to face him again; this time in front of two or three hundred people as part of the annual charity exhibition in August. The event would feature the best local professional players, alongside other big names and a "surprise guest". The prospect was incredibly daunting (understatement, especially considering my chronic fear of failure) but there was no way I was going to turn down the opportunity.

In the weeks leading up to the big night, I had done a fair bit of practising in front of a crowd of none in our garage, and without any pressure I'd done reasonably well: a few 180s and several games of 501 in 15 darts – and fewer on one or two occasions. Give me an audience, however, and I knew the fish would be swimming in an altogether different kettle.

Elaine and I opted for the VIP tickets for the exhibition, which meant we could get a free glass of something fizzy, a few nibbles from the buffet and seats that were too close to the stage for comfort. In addition to Glen, the other players on view included Middlesbrough-born Colin Osborne, Welsh international Jim Williams, "Rapid" Ricky Evans who threw as quickly as his nickname suggested, and the mystery guest, who turned out to be the former world number one and three-time world championship runner-up "One Dart" Peter Manley.

The second part of the evening would be devoted to the professionals, but the first half offered chances for some local players to have a game of 701 against one of the stars. Obviously there had to be a bit of a dip in proceedings, and that duly came when it was my turn in the spotlight. I'd spent a bit of time on the practice boards and had a quick chat with Peter Manley, who seemed like a decent bloke. And I was still scoring well – albeit in sporadic patches.

I was given a lovely introduction, but I was quaking inside as I climbed onto the stage to the strains of 'Sharp Dressed Man' by ZZ Top (I could have sworn I'd asked for 'I Missed Again' by Phil Collins). Elaine's final words were, 'Don't trip over the oche!' and thankfully my footing remained secure throughout.

The game got underway and after three darts each, I was actually in front; but the situation changed very quickly as Glen hit a string of good scores. The MC must hast have been getting fed up of starting every sentence with the words "one hundred and ..." after Glen had thrown (I know I was!), but the test for me wasn't in trying to compete, it was simply to stand up in front of all those people, with the memories of all the times darts hadn't even left my hand, and not embarrass myself.

I had dartitis and cripplingly low self-esteem – a symptom of my dysthymia – to contend with, and I just wanted to get up on stage and play a reasonable game.

And I think I did that – although it depends on your definition of "reasonable", I suppose!

After closing out on double four, Glen then took the microphone and said some very kind words about me and my challenges.

From that moment forward, we've stayed in touch.

As you've read, Glen supported both of my darts marathons, and he also came along to my 34km indoor row towards the end of 2016. He's a genuinely nice bloke and it was brilliant to sit in front of the television and cheer him all the way to the world title in January 2017.

CHAPTER 16

FIGHTING AN UNSEEN FOE

During the first quarter of 2017, I wrote online again about my dysthymia. I suppose I'd become used to trying to describe the effects of my condition over time, but finding the right words could still be really difficult on occasions.

Actually, I said "condition", but more accurately it is probably "conditions" – plural – given that I'm actually still prone to anxiety and panic attacks. Seasonal Affective Disorder pays an annual visit, which I always look forward to. I also look forward to opportunities to end a sentence with a preposition – which I now haven't.

Anyway, this is how I was feeling as an albeit mild winter was (or at least seemed to be) drawing to a close.

It's weird how some months seem to drag, yet fly by at the same time. On the one hand, it feels right that it's March already, but on the other hand the first two months of the year seem to have been a real slog – as they are most years, I suppose.

I'm really not a big fan of dark mornings and evenings, but I'm thankful that (thus far at least) we've had a fairly mild winter with only one snowfall of any significance. Of course, my half empty glass now assumes we'll get a wet summer by way of compensation ... but warm rain beats ice every time.

I do tend to withdraw into myself once the nights start closing in, which isn't so much of a problem at home (because I share my life with someone incredibly special), but it does mean numerous outings for my "work face". I'm lucky that I work in a supportive environment, but it's still very much part of my nature (and probably always will be) that I will try to hide the fact I'm struggling.

So far this year, every morning has started pretty much the same. I wake up feeling flat, usually after some version of recurring dream that I've been having since my late teens. I have vivid dreams every night without exception, and this particular dream reappears probably two or three times a week.

In the dream I am back at school. It is always the last day of term in my final year, but I haven't done enough work or revision for my exams. I'm almost certain not to have passed, and as everyone else leaves to prepare for the next stage of their life, I have absolutely no idea what I'm going to do ...

Dreams never seem quite so intense when you commit the content to paper. But when I'm asleep, my panic and dread quickly escalate to hopelessness – and the feelings are so strong, so real. When I wake up I feel mentally drained, yet I cannot deny that there is almost some bizarre sort of comfort in the "normality" of a dream I know so well.

Sometimes the heavy-headed negativity eases fairly quickly, yet there are days when it just lingers. And one of the worst things about my condition is that sometimes I almost want to feel low. I do have strategies to cope with, manage or reduce all the worst characteristics of dysthymia. And yet there are often things I feel a need to do to make sure the feelings persist.

That might sound ridiculous. It certainly looks ridiculous of paper, but there are times when it seems easier to simply accept feelings that I've known so well for so long – and wait until they inevitably pass.

This often feels easier than trying to find the strength for yet another fight with an unseen foe. Sometimes you have to pick your battles.

My mind often wanders on the way to work, and negative emotions fill my head. But thankfully I manage to keep the tears at bay. When I arrive, I seem to be ready to switch from introspective to work mode – only eight hours to not give away how I'm really feeling.

For so many years I didn't know what was wrong with me – and even when I finally realised, I stayed in denial because I mistakenly believed that admitting to any form of mental illness was to admit to weakness. I may not have fully come to terms with the fact that I have a mental health condition, but I am thankful that despite it being chronic, it is also mild.

Over recent years I've been able to get to know and understand myself and dysthymia pretty well. There are still times when I feel weak, others when I know I have to be strong. I don't think I'm brave, nor do I think I am a coward – at least, I hope I'm not. I am just me – contrasts, contradictions, flaws and all.

Dysthymia has undoubtedly made me who I am – or, to put it another way, I wouldn't be where I am today without dysthymia. So no, the past two months haven't been great, but even on the toughest day, I honestly wouldn't change the life I have.

CHAPTER 17

APACHE PERFORMANCE

DO A STAND-UP COMEDY ROUTINE
IN FRONT OF AN AUDIENCE

There were a number of times during the past few years when the prospect or reality of one of the challenges made me nervous.

But at precisely 21.36pm on Wednesday 3rd December 2014, I was officially petrified.

That was the moment when compère Allyson Smith introduced me to the audience, and I made the short walk onto the stage at The Stand Comedy Club in Newcastle city centre to make my debut as – and the clue's in the name of the venue – a stand-up comedian.

Trying to make an audience of strangers laugh, especially when they had paid for the privilege, was always going to be a massive test – of my nerves, my fear of failure, my ability (or not) to be funny.

I am definitely not a performer, and if anyone was to suggest that I was an extrovert, that would simply be down to the fact that I've learnt to hide the reality of my shyness.

So much could have gone wrong, but this was something I *had* to do.

In the lead up to the big day, I had been practising my "routine" in the car to and from work, making the odd adjustment here and there, and trying to ensure I could keep to my five-minute time limit.

The prospect of what was going to happen was daunting enough, but that was nothing compared to how I felt when I actually arrived at the club and saw the stage, with the nearest table and chairs no more than five feet away from the microphone.

Remembering lines while trundling along the A172 was one thing, but prospect was about to become reality, and it didn't take long for the doubts to start creeping in. Would I forget my lines? Would anyone actually laugh? Would I make a complete fool of myself?

The evening hadn't got off to the best of starts: £9.60 to park in a multi-storey that was due to close just after ten o'clock. You could have bought a bloody meal for two for that price ...

(Incidentally, you actually could: our bill in Burger King came to £9.58.)

Back in the club, Elaine and I sat at one of the tables near the front, and slowly but surely the room started to fill. After a while, I ventured into the "Green Room", which was actually a couple of sofas and a table in a small alcove, with walls covered in pages from comics. There were a few people in the room, so I did the sociable thing and introduced myself. They were all performing in the show, but I was the only first-timer (which didn't make me feel any better).

By now a few friends had arrived: Heidi (an old work colleague I hadn't seen in years), John (from the Gateshead football terraces) and Stephen – aka Kev – a former Gateshead Fell cricket teammate. I had a chat with each of them, and then suddenly realised that because of the noise in the room, I was having to talk louder than usual. And I was starting to lose my voice!

The show started at half past eight – another hour for me to wait. Allyson did an opening spot that went down well with an audience which, by then, had reached three figures. One by one the acts came and went, the standard seemingly getting better as the first half progressed.

I was first on after the interval, and I was getting more and more panicky by the minute. During the break, I found a quiet corner to have one last look over my script, and Allyson gave me some reassurance, as well as advising me just to concentrate on my opening line. If it went well, the rest would flow.

Apparently!

Allyson gave me a really nice introduction, and all of a sudden – with totally unexpected cheers and applause ringing in my good ear – there I was standing on the stage with a microphone in my left hand, with my right resting on the stand in a futile attempt to look calm and relaxed.

I could only see two rows of faces; the rest of the room was in total darkness, and I think that helped. My first shakily delivered line got a positive response and I was officially underway.

You may not necessarily agree, but I've been told it would be a really good idea to give you a flavour of the evening. I had three "stories", all of which were basically true, but let's just say I exaggerated them, and I was both amazed and thrilled that the punchlines got laughs and the puns got groans.

For the opening segment, I took the audience back to Christmas 1984, when I worked in the toy section of a large department store, and all the kids wanted to get their hands on *Star Wars* figures and models (following the release of *The Return of the Jedi*). The one figure that everyone really wanted was Princess Leia, but they weren't going to find it on our shelves – mainly because the box containing Alderaan's most famous royal resident had been extremely well hidden in the stockroom.

Apparently ...

Back on stage, I told how kids would frantically search for the elusive princess, allowing me to delight the audience with my almost legendary impressions: Obi-Wan Kenobi ("These aren't the figures you're looking for"), and Yoda ("Find Leia, you will not") – although sadly the latter sounded more like John Major than the diminutive Jedi knight.

The second story took place in an Italian restaurant and involved a man who had gone for a bite to eat shortly after getting off a long-haul flight. He fell ill after eating a pizza and was diagnosed with a deep-pan thrombosis ...

The third and final tale recalled a moment in the 2004 Great North Run (a half-marathon that starts in Newcastle Upon Tyne and finishes on the seafront in South Shields). After just over 10 miles, I was plodding along nicely and feeling reasonably strong – until I was overtaken by someone wearing a pineapple costume (this actually happened). All those hours of training just to be passed by a piece of tropical fruit!

Anyway, the story veered away from the truth when I also claimed to have been overtaken by someone running incredibly fast in an outfit shaped like a piece of cheese. I was so impressed by the pace of the cheese segment that I made a note to check the results and find out the name of the competitor – it was Gorgon-Zola Budd.

Despite what you've just read, the reaction I received at the end of my routine was amazing, so much more than I could possibly have hoped for. As I left the stage I saw Elaine, who looked so proud, and at that moment I was hit by a sudden surge of adrenaline – probably tinged with a hint of relief. As I made my way back to my seat, I walked past most of the other acts involved on the night, and received a warm handshake from all of them.

It felt fantastic: almost overwhelming.

Unfortunately, because the bloody car park was due to close, we couldn't stay until the end of proceedings, but even the delays we encountered on the journey home weren't going to detract from a truly memorable experience (although the £9.60 car park fee still rankled).

With your indulgence, here are a few comments from those who were there:

It was a joy to be part of your experience. Thank you! – Allyson Smith

I am so proud of you. – Elaine

Richard, very well done. That took some bottle, my friend. An unbelievable effort. I really enjoyed the night and you are a true inspiration. I salute you, mate. – John Young

I really enjoyed it, and you are definitely one brave man! Some people barely made an impression on the crowd, but you had us laughing the whole time. You have definitely inspired me to do more challenging things. However – seeing how scared you were beforehand (even though you didn't show it on stage) – I might need to start smaller than a stand-up gig! Thanks for inviting me; it was great to catch up. – Heidi Thompson

And finally, this review from Stephen "Kev" Devenport (it's actually longer than my routine!):

It was great to be there at Kirbs' latest challenge, and what follows is an eye witness account of events!

I can confirm that as the show started the realisation of what he had to do rapidly dawned upon him. The pressure was visible as he wrung his hands in the chair next to me, and audible as his vocal chords tightened. They began to fail him – and all this happened while he was still a member of the audience!

Having formed a friendship with Kirbs through playing the wonderful game of cricket, I'd seen these signs before. Usually I saw them as he was waiting for his turn to bat, but I had great confidence that he'd come through it – I knew he'd put his all into it as he always did on the pitch.

As the acts came on and the night got going, the quality of performance seemed to increase. Kirbs was questioning why he'd dropped himself in

this predicament! Time was now his tormentor; he wanted his moment in the spotlight never to come, but come it did.

Enter Kirbs stage left to deliver his material. And he certainly delivered. It was very satisfying to see him nail his first punchline and, as it was met with appreciation by the crowd, punch the air in celebration! The demons left him as he settled into his act.

For me, by far the most polished, funniest and genuine part of the piece was a joke Kirbs hadn't rehearsed or agonised over – one he hadn't spent hours reciting to himself or practising in front of the mirror.

He was performing a mime to embellish one of his stories and mistakenly (I think) mimed a young boy reaching down rather than up to take his mother's hand. To be honest, I don't think anyone in the room had noticed, but Kirbs had, and quick as a flash he quipped: 'He had a very small mother.'

Instantly the mask slipped and his panic at trying to remember a rehearsed script disappeared, to reveal a man who has genuine quick wit and the ability to produce comedy from nothing. That's the reason I'm mates with him!

Well done, Kirbs. It was a brilliant effort, and it was all the more pleasing that the audience got a glimpse of the real you too!

DO A STAND-UP COMEDY ROUTINE FOR MY MIDDLESBROUGH FANS!

Those five minutes should have brought down the curtain on what cannot even loosely be called my comedy "career", but I made the unwise (some would say foolish) decision to have another go.

The gig (technical term …) was held at the Westgarth Social Club in Middlesbrough. The venue was smaller than The Stand Up in Newcastle, but the stage was quite a bit bigger. The lighting was less intense, which was a blow … it is a whole lot easier when you can't see the people you're trying so hard to entertain.

There were two definite parallels with my debut the previous December: the more experienced performers were all very friendly and encouraging, and once again I was incredibly nervous.

The standard of acts was also very good … another blow. The three who were on before me all looked at ease behind the mic, and engaged really well with the audience. I, on the other hand, was worried about everything from remembering my lines to something as outwardly simple as how to stand without looking ridiculously awkward.

While trying to decide whether or not to take my drink on stage with me, I nearly missed my cue, but despite my all-too-obvious nerves the routine started well – the first punchline was rewarded with a few welcome chuckles.

The second story didn't really work though, and I was definitely thrown by one supposedly "funny" line getting no reaction at all. I stumbled through what unfortunately was the longest part of my routine, trying desperately to avoid more tumbleweed blowing across the stage, before things thankfully began to improve. The next two gags got a decent reaction, and the final "overtaken by a pineapple" tale (the one I was most comfortable relating) went down as well as I could have hoped.

I didn't get the rush of adrenaline that I'd had in Newcastle (and was desperately hoping to experience again), but that was undoubtedly down to the fact that one of my so-called jokes crashed and burned. For a split second, I didn't know what to do; my mind felt like it had gone blank, and getting through the routine left me with a feeling of relief rather than exhilaration.

In hindsight, I realised I was being hard on myself. I wasn't a performer and I wasn't a comedian. But not only did I have a go (strictly speaking, another go), I managed to recover from what was, for me, a really difficult moment. I finished the routine to the sound of laughter rather than silence.

When I decided to continue my challenges project into 2016, it was almost inevitable that one last attempt at stand-up would be on the list, because there was a lingering sense of unfinished business after the night at the Westgarth Club.

ROUND OFF MY COMEDY CAREER WITH A THIRD AND FINAL GIG

Whatever happened, the return to The Stand in May 2016 was always going to be my last performance – Elaine's orders – but nerves notwithstanding, I was determined to do my best and try to go out on a high.

My slot was at 8.54 (all very regimented), towards the end of the first half. I would have to say that the self-deprecating intro and selection of what I hoped were humorous one-liners were really well received. Nothing fell flat, and one "joke" (obviously in the loosest sense of the word) got applause ... actual real applause!!!

I will share it with you, but only on the understanding that the written version doesn't reflect the sublime quality of verbal delivery (or my ability to lie). Anyway, here goes:

"Some Native Americans are still relying on smoke signals to communicate after giving up on mobile phones, because they could only get *apache* reception ..."

© *Richard Kirby (Comedy Gold) 2016*

As my routine drew to a close, I told the audience that as they'd already guessed, I wasn't a stand-up comedian, and that I was on stage to try to raise mental health awareness. I'd made my debut at The Stand, and I was grateful to everyone who'd come along to the same venue to be part of my farewell.

The response was wonderful, and I felt fantastic as I returned the mic safely to its stand, gave a final wave and took my leave.

After I came off stage, one of the other acts actually asked why I was packing in, and several members of another 100+ audience came over to say they'd really enjoyed my "performance" (term used as per "joke" above). One even said I was "mint" – I'd never been called that before.

It was an amazing few minutes, made all the more special because Elaine was there with me.

GET INVITED BACKSTAGE AT A GIG

The introduction to this task comes from Neil "Mackie" McLennan, who (back in 1981) was the bass player with the punk band Blitz. Their 4-track EP *All Out Attack* (and specifically the opening song 'Someone's Gonna Die') not only had, but continues to have, a massive effect on me. What follows came from a chat back in late 2013 ...

We [Blitz] had been trying to get interest to get a record released. We had a little bit of press through Sounds Magazine, who were the only music paper interested in "Streetpunk" or "Oi" – oh, how we disliked that label. It was all just punk rock to us.

We had a full set of songs and decided to record the best four. Hologram studios in Stockport had an offer going on, where if a band block-booked a week's session, you could use the dead time – i.e. overnight, after the band or engineer had had enough, usually about seven, eight o'clock at night – for a reduced rate. So we went in for a couple of nights, and recorded and mixed in just two sessions, I think it was.

It was quite surreal to be stood on Stockport market, where the studio was based, at something like four in the morning, having a break from the studio – with the waft of Robinson's brewery in the air. So romantic!

It was a great time for us. What I always loved – and still do – is going in a room with an idea, knocking it into shape and coming out with a new song, and to get to hear them recorded was the icing on the cake for me.

It didn't matter if no one liked our stuff; we had written and recorded it and were happy just to have done that.

As far as the inspiration behind the EP, it's been pretty well documented that the early eighties were dark times for working class kids in the UK – the miners' strike, the three-day week, Tories fighting the unions, mass unemployment, you get the picture – and I suppose the songs were echoing the times. Listening back to the songs now, I realise there is a lot of violent imagery in them. There was a lot of violence around the punk scene back then, and this probably explains our mindset at the time.

We replied to an advert we had seen in Sounds for punk band demos, and sent the demo tape cassette. The advert was for No Future records and they wanted to put the four tracks out as an EP, just as we had recorded it, warts and all. We agreed and it became the first release on the new label. Sounds got behind it and we got great reviews. It enabled us to get decent gigs and got our name to places we never thought we would reach. It had no real impact financially, or to us as people at the time, but it did change people's view of us. And we didn't realise at the time just how far reaching our music would prove to be.

Back then the band meant everything to us. Cliché time again, but it was our way out. There were no jobs and we loved music and punk rock, so if we could use that to achieve something, then great stuff. Listening back to it now, it clearly sounds like a raw blast of sound, a warts-and-all recording of a moment in time. We did it quickly, on shitty gear, and pretty lo-fi – but that's what makes it.

The completion of the backstage challenge coincided with the first time I met Mackie, at a small gig at The Central in Gateshead, which featured The Slow Death (from Minneapolis, Minnesota), and Mackie's current band, Epic Problem. It was great to meet one of the quartet responsible for the hugely influential *All Out Attack* EP, and we were able to have a lengthy chat in the bar about all things musical. We also talked about my reasons behind the challenges before Mackie went on stage.

Despite having been involved with a band that had been a regular fixture at the top of the indie charts, Blitz never undertook a tour as such, and so this was a belated trek round the country that Mackie and the band were clearly enjoying. The "backstage" area looked very much like a pool room – due to the fact that there was a pool table in the room. Oh, and it said "pool room" on the door.

In an admittedly poor attempt to convince Elaine to come along, I'd told her it was a 60's tribute band night. It soon became blatantly obvious that it wasn't, although I was grateful to Epic Problem's frontman Jake for removing his shoes at the start of the set, and allowing me to draw an unlikely comparison with Sandie Shaw.

Epic Problem's final song of the night, 'Lines', was actually dedicated to both of us by Mackie. I'd never had a song dedicated to me before, and it was such a shame that I was in the toilet when this one was!

RECORD A SONG

Throughout my challenges project I'd had a go at things that I used to be reasonably good at, things I thought I might not be too bad at, and things I was hoping against hope I wouldn't be totally rubbish at.

Recording a song came very much in that final category.

True, I had been a chorister while at junior school, but my angelic treble tones disappeared in a flurry of teenage hormones, and I was left with a voice that would have been classified as basso profundo ... had I retained the ability to stay in tune.

That said, when driving to and from work with the window down and the volume up, I genuinely believed I could sing. It wasn't until I taped myself practising for this particular challenge that I realised that I couldn't have been more wrong.

It was a sobering realisation.

When I added the recording task to my list, I thought it would be a good idea to sing a duet, thereby offering me an opportunity to hide behind someone who had a much better and stronger voice. The Lee to my Peters came to me totally by accident, through a random conversation with a colleague at work (in early 2017). That colleague was Georgina Sayers.

It seemed like she was a talented singer, so I took the plunge and asked how she felt about singing with me if I was able to get everything arranged.

Georgina was aware of my dysthymia through some of the experiences I'd shared during events at work, but I was actually taken aback when Georgina said she would love to be involved. Although part of me suspected she'd only agreed because the likelihood of the plan reaching fruition probably appeared remote!

Even so, we chatted over possible suitable songs, and the final choice was one of Georgina's suggestions: 'Set the Fire to the Third Bar' by Snow Patrol (featuring Nancy Wainwright). I didn't know the song, but even on first listen, I really liked it. It was sung as a duet all the way through – perfect for hiding purposes – and although it was essentially of no consequence, I had seen Snow Patrol in concert sometime around 2000. That was shortly before they hit the big time, so I genuinely (albeit totally misguidedly) believed that that made me both trendy and relevant.

The next stage should have been the most difficult to finalise: finding a studio where we could record the song.

I decided to send an email to Lee Tuck, who I'd met a few times when he had been the bass player in an excellent rock band called The Karma Heart. I hadn't seen Lee for a good few years, but I thought he might possibly know someone involved with a recording studio who I could contact and ask for help.

Lee did know someone ... mainly because he had set up his own studio in South Shields a year or so earlier!

We talked through what I was hoping to do, and he said he'd be happy to get involved, not only to record the song, but also to video us as we were singing. He also wanted to shoot a short covering piece about my reasons for wanting to raise mental health awareness. It was an incredibly generous gesture; something that I could never have expected when I typed the original email. This all happened sometime in February 2017, but we decided to wait until early May before going into the studio because Lee was about to become a father. Oh, and I needed to practise!

The moment when I recorded myself (with such a dreadful result) came just two days before we were due to sing for real, and my nerves quickly escalated towards anxiety. But I tried to convince myself that Lee and Kyle Martin, his fellow director at the Garage Studios, would have state-of-the-art computer equipment capable of working miracles – even with voices like mine.

On the morning of 8th May, Georgina picked me up, and as we headed north up the A19 we sang the song together for the first time. As I suspected, Georgina had a lovely voice. But although I was still concerned about how I would sound, we both agreed that this was an experience we might never have again, and it was important to make sure we enjoyed it.

We arrived at the Garage Studios just before ten o'clock; Lee and Kyle appeared a couple of minutes later. We climbed the stairs and ventured inside ... and it all felt quite daunting. While Lee set up the lighting in the studio, Kyle was busy sorting out the backing track and all things technical. After setting up the studio, Lee joined Kyle in what I would have called the "control room"; they could talk to us, but we could not see them – and as far as my nerves were concerned, that was no bad thing.

Although we had both learnt the words, there was a copy of the lyrics on a music stand just in front of us, just in case one or both minds went blank when the recording got underway. We did a first run-though, which went reasonably well – except that I just couldn't find the right pitch for the opening notes of the first and third lines of the chorus. It was the one part of the song where the two voices diverged (if that's the right word) and harmonised. And, of course, I was conscious that there were two more choruses to come.

Georgina was very reassuring, just as I would have been had I been note perfect! I felt on edge (something that Georgina had picked up as well), but the second rehearsal was a bit better. The third attempt was recorded (audio only) and it was comforting when Lee came into the studio with a thumbs-up.

He then proceeded to position the three cameras: one that would have us both in view, and one pointing directly at each of us. Funnily enough, I didn't feel fazed by the cameras, nor the microphone. I just wanted to do my best and get the chorus right. We both seemed much more relaxed, and the first "take" (as we call it) went well – as did the second. By then I felt much less self-conscious and thoroughly enjoyed the live recordings. Georgina sounded amazing, and singing together was a lovely feeling.

Lee entered the studio once again, this time to say that they had everything they needed. Basically, they had two video- and three audio recordings and could use them to create the best overall finished product possible. They said it was just a case of cutting and pasting, but I'm sure it was a bit more involved than that. Either way, I hoped that I didn't irreparably damage their auto-tuning software, and I also encouraged them to consider auto-chinning software for future videos – sometimes one chin is all you want to see!

Lee then rearranged the cameras and lighting for the video, which I did in one take – and a 10-second introduction ... which took two! We took a couple of photos of the four of us and as the clocked ticked towards midday, the challenge was essentially completed.

Except, of course, that there was the small matter of the recording: how would we sound ... and what would we look like?

I was like a child on Christmas morning waiting for the files to appear in my inbox, but after hearing nothing for the rest of the day, a message from Lee appeared at just after six o'clock the following morning. I downloaded the files, then played the video ...

Oh wow!

It was amazing. Of course, I could easily pick all sorts of faults with the way I looked, but I thought the piece where I introduced myself and my story to camera definitely conveyed the message that it is fine to ask for help.

And the song just totally blew me away. However good I thought Georgina had sounded in the studio, the final recording was stunning. I cannot believe how lucky I was that she agreed to do this with me. I sounded far better than I imagined possible (don't you just love technology?). I was in tune, and actually our voices blended together really well.

Below is my introduction to the video – I'm sure it could have been more articulate, and the grammar could definitely have been better, but the message is definitely there. And even though I fluffed my first attempt at the introduction (which is just the opening sentence), I managed to get through the main section just like "One-Take Charlie" – if you remember him ...

You don't, do you? No matter. Here goes:

Hi, my name is Richard Kirby. I'm 52 and I'm from Middlesbrough, and I'm here in the Garage Studios in South Shields today to have a go at recording a song all about raising mental health awareness.

This all started off as a little challenge three and a half years ago, which was to set myself a list of tasks to do during the year I turned 50, and to try to raise a bit of money for the mental health charity Mind. It was only supposed to last a year, but three and a half years later we're still going. And today's challenge is number 86 out of a total of 100 that I'm hoping to complete by the end of the year. I'm not fundraising any more, but I'm working with the Time to Change project which is funded and therefore there's no donations. So now it's really just me helping to raise mental health awareness, showing that it's okay to talk about mental health, and show that it's absolutely fine to ask for help if you feel as though you need it.

Telling the story from my own personal point of view, I have a condition called dysthymia, or persistent depressive disorder as it's more commonly known nowadays. I'm lucky because it's a very mild condition, but it's also chronic, and therefore something I've probably actually had for around 40 years.

I remember the first time that I recognised that there was something significantly wrong with me and I went to the GP to ask for help. I didn't even get the first sentence out before I broke down completely. I was very lucky, though, because the GP was prepared to listen to me and he was prepared to help. And that's made a significant amount of difference.

These challenges have been done in such a way that I've had to ask for help for the vast majority of them, and quite often from people I don't actually know. So, in essence, there's a link in most of my challenges to my initial visit to the GP - who I didn't really know.

But the help has been out there. So many people have played such an important part in all of these challenges, in actually getting me to a position where I feel I'm making a little bit of a difference at least.

I have a few more challenges to do, obviously unless my recording career takes off after this! (Which is probably unlikely.) Challenges really do take up an awful lot of time, and preparations have been time consuming. I've driven in excess of 5,000 miles to get these challenges done. But the difference they've made to me and my life has been absolutely extraordinary, and I've met some incredible people - some really inspiring people - who've gone out of their way to give support to somebody who, in some cases, they'd never even met before. In a number of instances, people have stayed in touch and friendships have been made, and all because I have a mental health condition.

It's quite ironic, really, that a lot of the things I've done and the people I've met would never have happened to me if I didn't have dysthymia. And while I still have it, and while it's always going to be part of me and part of who I am, it no longer defines me.

So really I'm just trying to show that whatever you do, please don't be afraid to ask for help. Because it's absolutely fine.

It was all very surreal – especially listening to the audio. I knew it was me, but it was still hard to fully accept it. But for me, the day was all about Georgina, Lee and Kyle, without whom this challenge could not have been completed. What Lee and Kyle did was just fantastic, and the postscript that follows reinforces a feeling that I had within 24 hours of the recording: that this was the single most compelling and memorable challenge of them all.

My condition had never been hidden from my work colleagues, and when they were invited to watch the video immediately after a management meeting (which I obviously hadn't attended), the room was hardly buzzing with anticipation. I don't look great on a 7x5 photo, so seeing myself on a huge projector screen really wasn't very pleasant – so I took an executive decision and watched the floor. I was standing next to Georgina, and with the exception of one colleague who had guessed why we'd both been on leave the previous day, no one in the room knew what was coming. There was an audible murmur in the room, when our names came up on screen. We exchanged a glance and a nervous smile, as the first bars of the intro drifted across the room.

The next three and a bit minutes were totally bizarre, as was the round of applause at the end of the song. Just a few short minutes earlier, everybody would rightly have perceived us as just two workmates. But now we were workmates who had recorded a song together; something tangible, permanent and, as was becoming clear, something very special. Everyone we meet at work will have a hobby, interest, skill or talent that we know little or nothing about, and it must have been such a strange sight to see two familiar faces doing something so far removed from the day job.

We both received some really nice comments about the song. Quite rightly everyone loved Georgina's voice, but one or two were kind enough to suggest that I could hold a note or two as well.

A few minutes later I had to pop down to one of the other offices – cue another round of applause, and plenty of questions about how everything had been arranged and how we'd managed to keep everything a secret. I'm sure I looked as awkward as I felt, but I was genuinely thrilled (if slightly embarrassed) to get such a positive response.

That night, I uploaded the video and posted a couple of links on social media. I will readily admit that I was totally unprepared for the reaction. Notifications, comments and messages appeared throughout the evening, interrupted by an incredibly emotional phone conversation with my younger daughter. The response was unvaryingly positive, but as the number of views of the video passed 100, 200, 300 ... I could sense the whole experience was having a really powerful emotional effect on me.

I wanted to feel a sense of pride in what Georgina and I had achieved, but the reality was that I suddenly started sinking under a barrage of negative thoughts and feelings. After doing my best to come across as someone strong and confident, my mind picked that precise moment to remind me just how quickly my fragility could resurface.

Maybe that was the price I had to pay for trying to raise mental health awareness?

I'd lived with dysthymia for so long. And though I'd learnt it didn't always need a trigger to rear its ugly head, I suppose talking about my condition on a platform that was so readily accessible to basically anyone was – albeit inadvertently – an open invitation for intense and potentially overpowering symptoms to return.

The inevitable tears came – a sudden deluge on a drive to work. It was a bit of a relief in a way, because I didn't want anyone to see me in that state. I put my "work face" very much into good use over the next few days as I tried desperately to hide just how withdrawn I was becoming.

The hand was tightening its grip and all I wanted to do was cry. But out from the sadness I had experienced so many times came a frustration that verged on anger. I was angry that my mind just wouldn't let me accept I'd been part of something really positive.

With Elaine working regular late shifts, the opportunity just never arose to fully talk things through, and in the end I took out my pent-up emotion on an essentially inanimate object – a rowing machine. I smashed my 10km record by over two minutes on the Friday night, then shaved a similar amount from my 20km best the next morning. Physically I felt fantastic, and with Elaine's support over the weekend, I slowly gained back my emotional strength. I was ready to fight – and for once, the hand had nothing to offer in return.

Perhaps (hopefully without sounding overly dramatic) it was just one more battle in this interminably long war. But as much as recording a song was undeniably the defining challenge, maybe proving to myself that I was determined to fight was a defining moment on an altogether different level.

Singing with Georgina – the defining challenge.

CHAPTER 18

MRS K

My self-awareness about who I am as a person and how I am affected by my condition has increased almost exponentially over the past decade or so.

I couldn't have reached the point in my life where I'm comfortable talking openly about my own mental health without so much amazing support from my parents, children, family and close friends. But as you may already have guessed, it is my wife Elaine who has made (and continues to make) the biggest difference.

It's weird, but when I look back at my adult years before Elaine and I met, I feel like I just plodded along, almost existing rather than living. Obviously, starting again in our early forties was not without its challenges – be they emotional, financial or practical. Two marriages ended so we could be together and, regardless of the state of those respective relationships, we were always acutely aware that it wasn't just about us. What we were doing would also have far-reaching consequences for others ...

I told Elaine about my condition on our first date – ever the romantic – but when I moved down to Middlesbrough in the summer of 2006, I suppose I was still trying to fully come to terms with my diagnosis.

I had a fair idea about how my mild depression could affect me, but it really didn't matter how much I explained to Elaine – she was only ever going to get some level of real understanding when she actually saw me on a bad day. I can remember how shocked she was the first time I had a panic attack in my sleep. I don't get them all that often, and Elaine now knows that she just needs to encourage me to try to relax and breathe slowly, and tell me I'll be fine in no more than a couple of minutes.

But that first time, I think she jumped higher than I did!

As far as mental health is concerned, the defining moment in our relationship was undoubtedly the breakdown I had in that Birmingham hotel room in late 2011. I was in such a state, and just when I most needed to be with her, I was on my own, 170 or so miles from home. All I wanted was to go to New Street station and catch the first train north ... the fact that it was three o'clock in the morning was irrelevant. Hearing Elaine's voice was a comfort, but as soon as the phone call ended, I was battered by wave after wave of dark thoughts and negative feelings all over again.

By 7 o'clock, I was sitting in a coffee shop, having had another conversation with Elaine. I was still desperate to come home, but much as she said she'd support me whatever I decided to do, Elaine realised that there would be some repercussions if I failed to attend a course after work had paid for me to travel to Birmingham and stay overnight.

I felt so confused. The urge to go home was so powerful, but as the morning sunlight made its first appearance above the shops and offices on New Street, I realised I had to somehow find the strength to get through the day.

Luckily, a good friend from my office was on the same course, and when she saw me she immediately knew that I was struggling. We were able to have a quick chat before the course got underway, and a proper talk at lunchtime. It made a huge difference.

Elaine picked me up from Middlesbrough station later that evening. It was so good to see her and be able to hug her, but I remember that my overwhelming feeling was actually guilt. I knew I must have both worried and upset her, and that was actually bothering me far more than the fact that I'd dipped so badly. It was clear from the discussions that followed that Elaine didn't fully understand exactly what had happened: how and why I'd become so low, so quickly.

But how was she supposed to understand when I didn't even have any answers?

Thankfully, things improved over the next few days, and a reduction in my medication prevented any repeat of such an extreme reaction.

By my standards, I remained fairly stable for quite a while after that episode (over three years, in fact), but the knock-on effect is that you become almost used to feeling reasonably well. The next significant dip came during the summer of 2015. It wasn't anywhere near as bad as the one I'd experienced in Birmingham, but its effect was arguably heightened because it was so unexpected.

By now I'd started doing my challenges and sharing them with others to raise mental health awareness. Elaine and I had begun to talk more often about how introspective and low my condition could make me feel, and she had developed an ability to notice when I wasn't quite right – sometimes before I realised myself!

Now, if I have a really tough day, Elaine is able to reassure me that the worst of the feelings will pass. They're not simply words; she knows from experience it's only a matter of time before the negative thoughts ease away. She has always given me unconditional love and encouragement, but for me the most important thing is how *she* copes throughout and after the more difficult times.

Elaine is a quiet person and doesn't often give away how she is feeling, but whenever we talk about my condition, she always says that she loves me for who I am, and that dysthymia is simply part of who I am. She is well aware of the symptoms and effects, but she deals with everything in a totally unassuming and dignified manner. She insists that she has all the support she needs (even though I have the annoying habit of continually asking if she's okay).

For so many years, I did my best to cope with the effects of what I now know to be dysthymia – quietly, and on my own. I didn't realise how much energy it took to battle a mental health condition (and keep it hidden), until I had the chance to share my life with someone who was prepared to get to know the "real" me. Someone who believed I was worthy of her love.

I really am incredibly lucky.

CHAPTER 19

GIRL POWER

DO STEPHANIE FROM WORK'S MAKE-UP FOR HER

Steph had already been involved in the rollercoaster challenge, but during 2014 she also volunteered to let me do her make-up.

As the appointed day drew closer, Steph asked if I was intending to take the challenge seriously, or if it was simply an opportunity for some form of comedy face painting. The answer was very much that I was taking it seriously, as I casually dropped the black permanent marker on the floor and kicked it under the desk …

In fairness, I think Steph was more bothered about me wasting some of the contents of her make-up bag, the combined value of which would have seemingly paid for a pleasant week away in the sun.

Cometh the hour, I managed to persuade Steph to agree to a "before" and "after" photo by way of some sort of proof that she hadn't just applied the make-up herself. I'm not sure how much the pictures actually showed the extent of the difference, but it was apparent that it would have required me to mess up really badly to spoil her looks.

10 or 15 minutes (I wasn't going to be rushed) were taken up with my applying foundation, concealer, eye shadow (two lots, no half measures), mascara, lip gloss, etc. I don't know what was more impressive, me keeping a steady hand throughout, or Steph not flinching, especially when I was near her eyes. But not only did I actually enjoy the whole process, Steph was almost impressed with the end result ...

Well, that's what she said. Most likely she was just relieved.

GET A PHOTOGRAPH WITH A BEAUTY QUEEN

During the summer of 2016, I ticked off yet another of the meeting "challenges" – although in this case the word was something of a misnomer, given that it involved being photographed with a beauty queen. For the record, this was Gel Williams' idea ... and I was more than happy to accept such an excellent suggestion.

I had got in touch with Alexandra Devine, a director of the company which organised the Miss North Yorkshire competition (and a former Miss Tees Valley in her own right). Alexandra arranged for me to meet the recently crowned Miss North Yorkshire, Emily Austin, during a photoshoot at Solberge Hall near Northallerton.

The last beauty contest winner I can remember is Hólmfríður Karlsdóttir (the gorgeous but unpronounceable Miss Iceland), who won the Miss World title in 1985. She was born exactly one year earlier than me, so if my maths is correct, she should be about 35 now ...

Give or take.

In stark contrast, Emily was just 18 years of age. If that didn't make me feel old, the fact that she was 12 and eight years younger than my two daughters most definitely did.

When I arrived, Alexandra was getting ready to take a series of photos of Emily on an ornate chaise longue – just your average hotel furniture. We certainly don't have one in our house (at least we didn't the last time I looked). Alexandra took us outside (apparently grey hair photographs better in natural light) and after a quick chat, Emily and I posed for a few pictures taken with both my camera and Alexandra's – the latter being a slightly more impressive piece of equipment than my vintage instamatic!

There was nothing difficult about this challenge, but in hindsight, it was unusual insofar as this was only the second time I hadn't put my arm around my photographic companion – it just didn't feel like the appropriate thing to do. For the record, the previous occasion was when I met Boris the Golden Eagle …

I was pleasantly surprised when I saw the photos. Only one of us was ever going to look natural and relaxed in front of a camera – but I felt sure Emily would soon get the hang of it.

RECEIVE A LETTER FROM AN OSCAR WINNER

This chapter's final story is from 2017, and turned out to be one of the more memorable challenges.

There were a few British Oscar winners to choose from, including Dame Judi Dench, who was born in York (and so was I), Dame Helen Mirren, and the person to whom I eventually penned my request: Emma Thompson. There is actually a link between me and the dual-Oscar recipient, but it stretches the definition of "tenuous" to its very limit. I attended the same school as Emma's husband Greg Wise (who was known by his actual first name, Matthew, at the time). From memory, he was one year below me, but as my ability to deliver a line was about as good as his at delivering a cricket ball, our paths never really crossed.

But I mentioned it nonetheless …

Several months passed before a self-addressed envelope was nudged through the letterbox. It contained a lengthy handwritten note on a large postcard which featured a silhouette caricature of Nanny McPhee (the character first played by Emma in the 2005 film of the same name). I was both thrilled to receive the response, and moved by the emotion of Emma's words ...

Dear Richard

Thanks so much for your letter! Yes – I believe that mental health is just the same as physical health. We all have it and sometimes, just as in physical health, it needs attention / medication / counselling and all kinds of care. I think we're very primitive in our fear of being labelled mentally unstable!

You'll perhaps be relieved to hear that I've had bouts of depression and always talked about it – many people I know have suffered all kinds of mental pain and illness – but I don't make a distinction between them and those who have broken their leg or developed cancer. It's ALL CONNECTED. So great for you – brilliant to work for the recognition of something we all have – mental health, which is good / bad according to all sorts of reasons. Right behind you and sending admiration and good luck for the future.

With warmest regards and a big hug.

Emma Thompson + 2 Oscars!

Wow! Just wow!

CHAPTER 20

CHANNELLING MY EFFORTS

Sport has always been a massive part of my life, both as a participant and spectator. My first love is cricket, and I was lucky enough to play for a couple of fantastic clubs (Gateshead Fell and Chester le Street) during what I like to call a "career" that lasted the best part of 25 years. I took over a thousand senior wickets bowling my own brand of slow left-arm spin (minus the spin), and I also accumulated almost a couple of dozen runs with the bat.

The highlight was undoubtedly reaching the semi-final of the National Club Knockout in 1995, after a quite remarkable last-ball victory at Widnes in the quarter-final. Sadly, we lost to eventual winners Chorley in the last four, just one game away from a dream trip to Lord's. But since I was but a cricketer of only limited ability, it was a wonderful experience.

I always enjoyed playing badminton, and as I closed in on my 30th birthday I also started running – a slight misnomer given my lack of pace. That said, I did complete five Great North Runs between 1993 and 2005. One bizarre coincidence was that my best time of 2 hours, 23 minutes and 22 seconds was exactly the same (to the second) as my daughter Rebecca's finishing time in her first Great North Run in 2015.

As I've said before, eventually I was diagnosed with a chronic hip problem that brought to an end all my sporting activity of any intensity, but I managed the condition pretty well. By 2014 I was determined (if not totally ready) to take on some sporting challenges.

BOWL AT A TEST CRICKETER

The most appropriate starting point has to be cricket, and 10 years after that enforced retirement I set myself the challenge of bowling at a test cricketer.

Between 1969 and 2012, my father ran the first XI cricket at St Peter's School in York. The previous incumbent, Robert Harding, had done the job since the end of the Second World War, which meant that just two men had overseen the main summer sport for a period of 67 years!

I did once ask Dad (who had captained both Cambridge University and Leicestershire in the early 1960s) if he was to rank all the players from four decades into some sort of order, where would I come? Apparently, he had given it some thought – and I wasn't in the top 200 or so. Maybe I should have been a bit more specific.

How about just among the bowlers?

Left-arm bowlers?

Slow bowlers?

Bowlers called Kirby?!

Finally, I made it into the top 20!

Right at the very top of the list, however, was Jonny Bairstow, and it was perhaps fitting that the school's first future post-War test debutant came towards the end of Dad's tenure. Jonny's ability and potential were obvious from a very young age, and I know how thrilled Dad was when he came through the Yorkshire county ranks to become a full international.

Anyway, in May 2014, the 1981 St Peter's captain (me) met his 2007–8 counterpart (Jonny) at York Cricket Club so that I could complete the challenge.

After so long away from the game, I found it slightly unnerving trying to propel a ball from one end of the net to the other (preferably bouncing just once, and hitting the back of the net and not the side or top) with the cream of local cricketing talent warming up next to me.

That said, the first ball not only pitched, it turned as well; from memory that had last happened in 1998 – and even then it was only the once. Anyway, I practised for about a quarter of an hour before Jonny arrived, and it was time to bowl the "proper" over.

All six pitched (once each), the first four were slightly short of a length, but there was nothing wrong with the last two, which were very respectfully defended. I was pleasantly surprised with how I bowled, although I was far less impressed by how much my back was starting to hurt (and did so for the next 48 hours!).

I took the customary picture and Jonny also signed another photo (which he duly pierced with one of his spikes for authenticity!). It was over in a matter of minutes, but they were the last deliveries I will ever bowl. It was a privilege to bowl them at arguably the finest player to have ever graduated from the St Peter's cricket field.

COMPLETE THE EQUIVALENT OF AN ENGLISH CHANNEL CROSSING ON A ROWING MACHINE

This was definitely one of my most physically demanding challenges.

The shortest distance between the English and French mainland is the 34km (21 miles) between Dover and Cap Gris Nez – and this was therefore my target. I joined the gym at Eston Leisure Centre in September 2016, and gave myself three months to train for the event, which was scheduled for 23rd December. This would allow me enough time to recover and regain the strength I would need to open all my presents on Christmas morning.

After my first couple of sessions on the rowing machine (or ergometer – "Erg" to its friends), a few things were apparent:

I was old, I was not very fit, and France was (and probably still is) much further away from England than it looked on a tiddly map.

I had sent an email to British Rowing to explain what I was doing and ask if they could offer some guidance on how best to prepare for the event. A few days later, I received a message from Neil Dunning, club captain of Tees Rowing Club, who said he would put Julian Bunn in touch with me, as Julian would be perfectly placed to help me with all aspects of the training.

At the time, Julian was one of the best indoor rowers of his age group in the whole country, and he had produced outstanding performances across various distances in competitions at home and abroad. Basically, he had forgotten more than I would ever know about indoor rowing and I was delighted that he was willing to work with me.

Ready to set off for France!

By the time we met, I had managed to extend my longest training session to 18km – just beyond halfway, and therefore too late to turn back. Julian helped me devise a structured training plan that would enable me to complete a 25–26km row a week or so before race day. This included recovery sessions and weights to make sure I was balancing the work being done by the muscles most used on the machine. He gave me tips on nutrition (and my ears definitely pricked up at the sound of the words "Jaffa Cakes"), along with plenty of valuable advice on hydration.

We talked about mental preparation which would be every bit as crucial as the physical training, and we exchanged regular emails as the work intensified.

Apart from a two-week hiatus caused by a particularly nasty virus that kept me away from both work and the gym, training went pretty well. I was aware that there would be good and bad days, and as fantastic as I felt after a 26km row on 11th December, I was equally sluggish over a much shorter distance the following Sunday. Overall though, I felt strong – but as with any endurance event, there would be difficult moments along the way, which was where the training and mental prep would come into play.

The toughest part of the training hadn't actually been the fitness, but the discomfort caused from sitting on the plastic seat for an extended period. I had devised a plan whereby I would row for 12–15km then use a padded seat to get me through to 20km, before discarding it again when the discomfort turned to pain.

I'd cramped quite a lot in the early stages of training, and that led to another concern, as too much liquid to overcome the cramp would lead to unwanted calls of nature. It took me almost the full three months to finally get the balance right.

Although the final five days prior to the event were essentially a time for rest, I went down to the gym on the eve of the race to record a piece with Louise Hobson of BBC Radio Tees. Louise had to use her phone for the recording after her tablet chose a particularly inopportune moment to stop working – an important reminder for me to check the battery in the rower, as a flat battery would equal no proof of completion.

I didn't sleep very well that night. I had prepared well, but my head was filled with the things that could go wrong (the battery, a painful posterior or an uncomfortably full bladder … or worse still, all three).

Thankfully, when I arrived, the leisure centre manager Rachael Gage was on hand to make sure everything was set up and ready. Julian duly appeared, followed soon after by Louise and her temperamental tablet. Warm-up and stretches complete, there was time for a short live chat with Louise (whose producer had apparently commented on my "nice legs" – presumably followed by "shame about the …"). I got a few last words of encouragement from Julian and off I went.

As the white Kentish cliffs disappeared into the virtual distance, I had a visit from my friend Glen Durrant, soon-to-be BDO World Darts Champion. Glen stayed and chatted for a while, and at various intervals during the row Louise would take short videos, during which I would give an update on my progress. Both she and Julian stayed for the whole event (which was massively appreciated). Gel Williams and Les Harrison also popped in to see how things were going. Elaine arrived fashionably late just before 11 o'clock, only to be persuaded by Louise to make her radio debut. Louise chatted to her and to Julian in a live feed just after half past eleven, before she came over to ask how close I was to la côte de la France.

If I'd maintained my pre-race plan of a steady 25 strokes per minute and a kilometre every six minutes, I would have been maybe four kilometres away, but almost certainly due to the hugely positive effect of the company, I'd been rowing faster than I'd ever done in training, and was only 200 metres from the finish.

Louise wondered how I was feeling. I said I was fine.

I was lying.

As I later learnt, the show's host stayed with Louise because I was so close to completing the 34km. I really pushed the last 100m and my finishing time of 3 hours, 1 minute and 21 seconds was a total surprise. It might not compare with anything a decent athlete could achieve, but I was so happy with what I'd accomplished, grateful for the coverage Louise had given the event, and indebted to Julian for his support and wise words.

It wasn't until afterwards that Julian admitted that he'd been worried that I hadn't given myself enough time to do the training required for such a long row, but this was his reaction during his on-air conversation with Louise: 'I cannot believe what this lad's just done. I have a couple of emails at home that told me what his splits were in some of his training sessions, and I don't think Richard's aware of it, but he's going half a minute per mile faster this morning, over 34k, than in his training sessions ... which were shorter. That is awesome. That is actually astonishing. He's working extremely hard, but he hasn't stopped talking! Staggering. Absolutely staggering. All credit to him.'

Louise then asked about my technique ...

'His technique hasn't changed. He's actually got quite good technique here. He's been so consistent all the way through, and he hasn't let his body collapse. One of the things we say about the long distances is that it isn't the day that matters, it's the training beforehand. It's the training that's hard. This has been hard, but he'll have enjoyed this when he finishes.'

One thing was for sure – I enjoyed the Jaffa Cakes!

REPEAT THE CHALLENGE BUT THIS TIME IN LESS THAN THREE HOURS

I took a bit of a rest from the gym after that; in fact, it took about three months before I felt the time was right to get back on the seat and start training again. There were two main motivations for me; one was the desire to shed a few pounds and the other was an increasing irritation that I hadn't broken the three-hour barrier, even though I was only really concerned with completing the distance at the time.

Throughout April and May I trained hard, and was rowing on average 40-50km every week. I wasn't working to any particular plan or timescale to have a second attempt at the Channel crossing, but the morning after my 53rd birthday I just felt ready. I had no publicity, radio, company or support this time (I would have to rely on social media and my website to announce the achievement) – there was just me, my mp3 player (my limit as far as technology was concerned), and a vast expanse of imaginary water.

Rowing such a long distance with no conversation or encouragement was every bit as tough as I expected, but I was much stronger than I had been a few months earlier and was just ahead of three-hour pace all the way through. I had a dip around 25km, but managed to maintain a decent rhythm (I was now used to rowing at 23 strokes a minute) and got my second wind around 30km – luckily there was no one on the treadmill behind me at the time.

For no particular reason, I took off my headphones for the final four kilometres, and eventually completed the 34km in ... wait for it ... 2 hours, 56 minutes and 19 seconds.

Job done!

As far as the rowing was concerned, if there was any element of competition, it was essentially against myself, or perhaps the clock. But the nature of the contest obviously changed completely with the introduction of an opponent. It didn't really matter whether or not I was a technically competent rower, so long as I was fit enough to reach the proverbial finishing line.

But in one-on-one competition, a lack of competence was clearly going to be exposed – especially when the opponent was an elite athlete.

PLAY TABLE TENNIS AGAINST
AN ENGLAND INTERNATIONAL

The likes of Rhys Walker and Jenny Wallwork were always going to beat me, but at least there was a sense of familiarity about stepping back onto a badminton court. The same was also true (albeit to a lesser degree) with table tennis, a sport I had played and enjoyed a great deal when I was at school.

Playing an England table tennis international turned out to be my 85th completed challenge, and I did it in March 2017. It was very much a trip down memory lane as, until a month before I played Danny Reed, I hadn't picked up a bat in over 30 years.

I went to three practice sessions at Ormesby Table Tennis Club (just a couple of miles up the road), and I have to admit I really enjoyed them. Obviously, I had lost a lot of the speed and movement that I never had in the first place, and as well as badly worn hips, I was also the owner of a left shoulder that would often click. But despite my physical constraints, my competitive edge returned almost immediately – and it felt great.

Ormesby had a team that played in the Premier Division of the British League, and Danny Reed was the ideal opponent in that he was not only an England international but also the winner of three Commonwealth medals: silver in the men's team competition in both Delhi and Glasgow, and bronze in the 2014 mixed doubles.

As well as clearly being a fantastic player, he was just over half my age, so it's safe to say the outcome of the game was never in any doubt. I felt quite nervous beforehand, but a reasonable number of shots found the table on Danny's side of the net, and soon it was game time. The table was set up for that afternoon's match against Cardiff City. There was a scoreboard and even a scorer ... and things started well when I won the toss to serve first.

I should probably have quit while I was ahead.

My aim was to not embarrass myself, and maybe play a shot good enough to win a point. At 10–0 in the opener, neither goal had been achieved, but I did win the next point – mainly because Danny deliberately put a bit more air on a return, to give me the chance of hitting a blistering forehand. Well, a forehand anyway.

What felt like moments later, Danny was 10–1 up in the second game too. That became 10–2 after my best point of the match (yes, I know there weren't many to choose from). Danny's one and only false shot took the score to 10–3, and to be honest he was on the ropes at that point – even though I don't think he realised.

The match was officially best of five, which translated as 'How long will I last before losing 3–0?' The answer was not much longer, and it did start to look like my side of the scoreboard was broken because the number never seemed to change.

On match point, I contrived to top edge a smash into the roof, and that was that: a straight sets defeat 11–1, 11–3, 11–1 to one of the best players in the country.

Danny's thoughts and movements were speedy, his forehand smashes lightning quick. I hadn't a clue what to do with his serves, but it was a great experience.

A fortnight later, I returned to watch Danny in "proper" action against North Ayrshire, and there was a nice moment after the opening game in his first match, which Danny won 11–2. As he walked past me, I mentioned that I'd managed more points in one of our games. Danny grinned and said he'd been thinking exactly the same!

SPAR WITH A PROFESSIONAL BOXER

This task takes us back to October 2014, when I travelled over to the Natural Progression Boxing Academy in Stockton-on-Tees to tackle a challenge which was worded thus: to train with a professional boxer.

The young man in question was Josh Leather, an unbeaten and highly regarded super-lightweight from nearby Guisborough. His trainer was none other than my friend Imran Naeem, who decided to alter the challenge from "train" to "spar". Some friend ...

Even though I didn't know what Imran had in mind, I was already slightly apprehensive when I arrived at the gym. Imran was putting a very impressive group of youngsters through their paces and, not for the first time during the first 12 months of the challenges, I felt every single one of my 50 years. Josh arrived, taped up his hands (I couldn't possibly tell you what he uses for padding) and started to warm up for his training session. Imran laced up my gloves before taking the pads and giving me my first ever boxing lesson. Despite my being slow of movement with the weakest right hand jab in history, the old "Kirby left" managed to connect a couple of times.

But still, Imran's declaration – after about five minutes – that I was "ready" was the very definition of misplaced confidence!

There were two main reasons why the original task was simply based around training. Firstly, I would never have insulted a professional athlete (or the other youngsters at the gym for that matter) by suggesting that a total novice like me could – or should – climb into a boxing ring. Secondly (and probably more importantly, if the truth be told) I wasn't exactly thrilled at the prospect of getting hurt!

That said, there was no way I was going to back out: I was fitted with a headguard and clambered rather clumsily into the ring (which was smaller than I imagined, and didn't seem to have an emergency exit).

Was I nervous? Too right I was. I was in a boxing ring with one of the best young fighters of his weight in the country ... about to attempt to spar for three one-minute rounds. And much as I realised Josh wasn't going to unleash his hardest shots, he wasn't going to simply move around the ring and let me try to hit him either. I wasn't wearing a gumshield, and I was happy to accept Imran's assurances that Josh wouldn't punch me in the mouth.

Bad mistake ...

Towards the end of the first minute, I attempted a pretty feeble combination, and the next thing I knew the inside of my upper lip was cut, my mouth was stinging, and Imran was laughing. I thought my gloves were up; evidently they weren't, and I honestly never saw the punch coming. I got tagged a few more times over the next couple of minutes, a second one in the mouth, one in the right eye and another to the side of the head. I quickly realised I needed to watch for Josh's right hand ... so I did, but it didn't make any difference!

It was hard to imagine just how hard Josh could actually punch, but his hand speed was incredible. His professional career was clearly on a sharp upward curve, but for me the only option was immediate retirement. I knew I'd been rubbish, but in truth that didn't matter. Not taking on the challenge would have been a whole lot easier than actually going through with it ... and I was actually quite proud of myself for having a go.

(Postscript: in May 2017, Josh became the IBF Intercontinental Super-Lightweight Champion with a sixth-round stoppage victory over Philip Sutcliffe Jr.)

GO CLAY PIGEON SHOOTING

Time for a little bit of shooting and running.

This challenge took place in the latter part of 2016 near Trimdon (the former parliamentary constituency of Tony Blair), which lies in County Durham, roughly 10 miles from Hartlepool.

Elaine and I were driven up to a very muddy farm by John Waite (a former work colleague of Elaine's) for our first attempt at clay pigeon shooting. Neither of us had ever held – let alone fired – a shotgun, but John took plenty of time to show us how to hold the gun, how to load it, aim it, fire it, discharge the cartridges and most importantly of all, how to do all of those things safely.

It was all well and good watching an expert making everything look ridiculously easy, but the reality became apparent when it was our turn. We were both well aware that hitting a tiddly little flying plastic disc would be incredibly difficult – and we weren't wrong.

I was actually very good … at shouting 'Pull!' But sadly, my first few attempts hit nothing but thin air, as clay after clay returned to terra firma in the same pristine condition in which they'd been projected skywards. Elaine's turn …

John helped her adopt the proper position, which Elaine duly adapted into her own stance – a stance which saw her propelled backwards into John's safe arms when the gun recoiled. John even managed to catch the ear defenders that fell off Elaine's head as two more discs floated gently, unscathed, back to earth. I shouldn't have chuckled, but I did. Elaine's riposte was to shatter one of the next clays into a thousand fragments!

John had a couple of guns with him, but I couldn't hit anything with either of them. The reason soon became evident when I was given the chance to try a left-handed gun. I was given a few more pointers about where to aim, and a few shots later I clipped the edge of a clay and deflected it away to the right. It wasn't as dramatic as Elaine's, but it was a hit nonetheless. A couple more misses followed, but then another hit … and another … then another … and then a fourth in a row. No one was more surprised than me.

The impassive young lad who was operating the trap then gave me what I understand was (for him) a massive compliment. He said, 'Not the worst I've seen, for a first attempt!'

We had no expectations of being any good – which was just as well. But we both enjoyed ourselves and managed to break our clay pigeon duck (very clever use of the "double bird").

RUN 2 MILES AT GATESHEAD
INTERNATIONAL STADIUM

Towards the end of 1992, I decided that I really wanted to have a go at the Great North Run. It's safe to say I wasn't a long-distance runner (or a short-distance one, come to think of it), and the prospect of completing 13.1 miles was daunting to say the least. I can clearly remember my first training run, when I managed about four hundred yards before my chest started burning, and I started to wheeze like an octogenarian smoker. It was embarrassing; even the blue-rinsers dashing for the bingo could comfortably outpace me.

I persevered and eventually completed five half-marathons before my hip problem was discovered. I hadn't jogged since the diagnosis, so it was with significant trepidation that I stepped out onto the track at Gateshead International Stadium in August 2014 to attempt a two-mile run.

I know it doesn't sound far, but equally I was well aware that every step could be the one when one (or more) joints gave out and the challenge would be over. I did some stretches, walked half a lap and jogged a few yards to see if the old magic was still there.

It was.

For about 300 yards!

In fairness, my legs and hips lasted longer than I expected. It very much had shades of 1992 and I had that breathlessness from being totally unfit. It was baking hot too, which didn't help, but I made sure I was sensible, drinking and pouring water over my head at regular intervals.

The last time I'd run on this track, I was training for the 2005 run – and did 20 laps in 42 minutes. I've heard it said that the stadium is a "fast track" – well, that certainly didn't apply to the lane I was in! There were no adoring crowds to cheer me across the finishing line, but equally there were no shouts of, 'Just shove him out of the way, Beryl! The number 24's coming and it's "eyes down" in 20 minutes!'

CHAPTER 21

DEPRESSION DOESN'T PICK AND CHOOSE

During the summer of 2011, BBC Radio 5 Live broadcast a programme highlighting the issue of depression in sport, focusing mainly on cricket. And given that the previous chapter was sport related, now seems like the appropriate time to briefly consider the effects of mental illness on those who play a sport I love at the highest level.

Part of the programme focused on a former Sussex and England cricketer named Michael Yardy, who had flown home from the 2011 World Cup (which was being hosted by India, Sri Lanka and Bangladesh) reportedly suffering from depression.

Although mental health was becoming more openly discussed, it was evident that there was still a fundamental lack of understanding of the effects of depression. On hearing about Yardy's situation, Geoff Boycott (ex-England opening batsman turned media pundit) suggested that the all-rounder was depressed because he wasn't good enough to be in the international one-day side, and the reason he himself had never suffered from a similar illness was because he was a far better player.

His comments were probably borne out of ignorance rather than malice, and a retraction of sorts swiftly followed.

But the fact is, depression is an illness which doesn't pick and choose its victims according to social status, wealth or sporting ability.

The case of Somerset batsman Marcus Trescothick brought the whole subject to public attention because he was, without doubt, one of the finest test players in world cricket when, in 2006, he quit an overseas tour to return home. There was an "old school" theory that playing for your country is an honour, and therefore Trescothick should have just got on with it. But illness or disease does not have to be visible to have incredibly debilitating effects.

While I believe that certain people may be predisposed to the condition, there may also be a link or a trigger in the game of cricket because of the length and nature of the game. The higher the level, the greater the demands (both on and off the field) and the more time you spend with teammates. Obviously, this means less time with family.

Does that bond between teammates become a dependency that can have serious health implications – especially when the bond is broken by retirement?

Being in a dressing room in the company of friends and teammates – possibly for many years – is a great experience even for a club cricketer like I was (or tried to be). When you stop playing though, that's that. You can never go back or recreate the feeling you enjoyed so much for so long.

And the relatively recent suicides of Mark Saxelby and David Bairstow are testament to some degree of the difficulty players can have adjusting to "normal" life. Bairstow's passing remains particularly poignant because I have had the pleasure of meeting, and even bowling at, his son Jonny while watching him develop into one of the finest wicketkeeper-batsmen of his generation.

Jonny's equivalent in the England women's side is Sarah Taylor, arguably the most gifted female cricketer in the country at the time of writing. Yet as recently as 2016, Sarah announced she was taking an indefinite break from the sport after suffering from debilitating anxiety attacks, sometimes while on the cricket field. It was much more than simply nerves, and while I can relate to panic – even dread – at the prospect of playing a game I'm supposed to enjoy, I cannot begin to imagine how magnified those feelings could be when you're playing at the pinnacle of the sport.

During the time I played cricket, I suffered from what is commonly known as the "yips" (a loss of fine motor skills, a condition also recognised in other sports including golf and darts). It happened three times: in 1982, 1994 and 1997, and all three episodes left me questioning whether I should, or could, continue playing.

The first occasion was during a North of England trial while I was still at school. It was a big deal at the time, and there were some good players on view (future England fast bowler Devon Malcolm among them), but I felt reasonably comfortable ... until the first net session. I ran up to bowl and the ball slipped out of my hand and hit the roof of the net. It had never happened before, yet in that single moment, I crumbled mentally.

All these people were watching. I was supposed to be reasonably good ... why hadn't I let go of the ball properly? What if it happened again?

If it does, I'm going to look stupid. If it does, I've failed ...

The next ball bounced twice ...

It took quite a while to get over that humiliation, but although I continued playing occasionally after leaving school, I didn't take the game seriously again until 1988. By that time I'd moved to Gateshead and joined the local club (Gateshead Fell). Although my nerves never fully left, I did reasonably well over the next few years, and had a decent season for the first XI in 1992. But if I thought I was free of the yips, I was taught a cruel lesson during a cup tie in 1994 – when, totally without warning, I lost the ability to let go of the ball.

Even typing the words brings back memories of overwhelming panic. This wasn't a practice session, it was an actual match ... people were watching the game ... watching me ... and I couldn't bowl. I honestly had no idea how I was even going to finish the over. I didn't want to bowl. I didn't want to be on the pitch ... not then, not ever again.

I can't really remember much about how my teammates reacted. I doubt any of them realised the extent to which my mind was being tortured by what had happened. I took a week off and spent time going back to basics, going through repetitive bowling drills, just trying to regain the tiniest bit of confidence in myself. Interestingly, the turning point came with a call asking me to represent the full league side. In fairness, the call only came because the game was being played at my home ground, and all the other slow left-armers in the area were for some reason unavailable.

My first reaction was to decline. I should have been excited at having the opportunity to play for a representative side, but the thought genuinely terrified me. But in the end, I found some inner strength and accepted, on the basis that realistically I would never be asked again. I practised for hours in the hope that I could hold it together on the day.

We fielded first and I came on to bowl quite early in proceedings. The only thing in my mind was to get the ball to the other end. *Just let go of the ball ... you've done it thousands of times before, you can do it now ...*

And the first ball was fine, as was the second. But the self-doubt lingered. Every delivery was the one that could go wrong ... and I just couldn't get that thought out of my head.

Then suddenly, the batsman took a wild swing and hit the ball miles in the air. It was my catch ... I got in position ... steadied myself ... watched the ball ... and *missed* it completely (to the extent that it hit me full on the chest). Yet again I just wanted the ground to swallow me up, but then something happened.

A teammate came over and told me in no uncertain terms what he thought about the dropped catch, but that I was good enough to be in the side, and now needed to show some fight. Normally that would have reinforced the negativity swirling round my head, but this time (and I can't explain why), I got angry. Not at the comments, but with myself. Two balls later I dismissed the batsman I'd dropped ... and it felt fantastic.

I was far from cured, but the fact that I remember the moment so vividly almost a quarter of a century later shows just how important it was. By 1997, I had joined Chester le Street Cricket Club. Two games into the season, I had taken nine wickets for the first XI, and the local paper contacted me to ask for an interview.

Within a fortnight the yips returned with a vengeance. It was almost as if my mind wouldn't allow me to succeed.

I travelled through to the ground almost every evening for the next couple of weeks, working either on my own or with one of the club's coaches, to try to find enough confidence and belief to get back out on the field. I managed to get through what was the final really bad episode, but there were still occasions when the prospect of bowling made me so anxious that I physically couldn't swallow. Thankfully I was a pretty ordinary fielder and was usually far enough away from the action to hide what was happening.

I realise it sounds almost ridiculous that you should put yourself through an emotional ordeal for the sake of game you play for fun. But even though my self-doubt was always close to the surface, I'm glad I persevered. I had so many brilliant times with some great people before age caught up with me and I retired in 2004 (literally months after my original diagnosis of depression).

I have so much respect for the likes of Marcus Trescothick, Michael Yardy and Sarah Taylor – as cricketers, but even more as people. I didn't have anywhere near their ability, but I now have some level of understanding of the way the mind can affect – or even control – the body. In an age when sport is driven by money and success, these stories show that behind the professional front, there are *real* people with *genuine* issues, and the benefit of radio programmes (and other media coverage) devoted to raising awareness of mental health in sport simply cannot be underestimated.

CHAPTER 22

TIME, SPACE, ACE AND GRACE

This chapter is dedicated to challenges involving my all-time favourite television programme: *Doctor Who*.

My first ever professionally published book, *Desperately Seeking Susan Foreman* (which went on sale in 2013) was a personal history of the programme, based around the search to obtain a signed photograph from all the female TARDIS companions from 1963 right through to what was present day (i.e. up to and including Clara).

Compiling the book was a thoroughly enjoyable experience, and the publication of the third edition was most definitely a long-time ambition fulfilled. The book's release led to a surprise invitation to attend an event called "Who's in the Library" towards the end of 2013. The library in question was in Mansfield, and although it was a 250-mile round trip, I had never done a book signing before. I went on the basis that I would probably never get asked again ...

Elaine made the trek down to Nottinghamshire too – just so that there would be one person in the building that had actually heard of me! The special guest at the *Doctor Who*-themed afternoon was Nick Briggs, most recently the man behind the voice of the Daleks. We received a warm welcome and Joanne, who had organised the event, had arranged a table and lovely little display for me.

I had no idea what to expect, but beforehand I had told Elaine that selling 10 books would be more than I could have hoped for. After 20 minutes I would have settled for selling one book, because nobody seemed to notice my little stall. But then came some interest, a bit of a chat, and a sale!

And then another, and another. Three books – that was the petrol cost covered. One more book and we could get a bite to eat too!

I would guess there were about 150 people at the event, including a few dressed as various incarnations of the Doctor. Plenty of people came over for a chat, I was even asked to sign a few autographs. I did try to talk my way out of it, but they absolutely insisted. In all, I sold 11 books. That would be nothing for an established author, but I was genuinely thrilled.

A few short weeks later, my challenges were underway and the first task on the list relating to Gallifrey's finest was to meet a companion.

MEET A CURRENT OR FORMER
DOCTOR WHO COMPANION

This task was duly completed in March 2014, with a first ever visit to a science fiction convention. I had no real idea what to expect, apart from a line-up of celebrity guests from various sci-fi films and television series and the likelihood of a fairly lengthy wait before being able to gain access to the Newcastle Arena.

Before setting off for the 50-mile drive, I had read a news report which said that the previous day's attendance – at what was the region's first convention of this size – had been so large that some people had queued for several hours. Others had been unable to get in, even with pre-purchased tickets.

When I arrived, there were queues stretching down both sides of the arena. Those at the front of the respective queues had arrived as early as half past six! Thankfully, once the doors opened, the wait was nowhere near as long as I'd anticipated. I went in search of Sophie Aldred, who had played the companion Ace back in the late eighties.

Among those sitting waiting patiently for visitors to appear at their respective tables were the now late Kenny Baker (R2-D2 in *Star Wars*) and David Prowse, who was the very embodiment of ruthless intergalactic domination in his guise as Darth Vader.

Primeval and S Club 7's Hannah Spearitt was there. *Indiana Jones* stalwart John Rhys-Davies and *Torchwood's* Kai Owen were among the others I recognised too, but I soon found the queue to see Sophie – and much to my surprise, I was second from the front. I had written to Sophie to mention the charity challenge. She'd replied and so hopefully it wasn't a total shock when I introduced myself – and gave her a copy of my book. We had a brief chat and not only did Sophie pose for a couple of photos, she also invited me round to her side of the table, presumably to sample the now legendary Kirby hug.

Or maybe not.

We couldn't talk for long, because there were plenty of others who wanted to meet Sophie, but she asked me to pop back when it was quieter. So I did ... twice!

The second time, we had the chance to talk for about 15 minutes, and *Doctor Who* barely got a mention! On the basis we had never met before, the conversation was fascinating and much more personal that I could have expected. At the time I was only a dozen or so weeks into the project, so to be stood discussing various aspects of mental health with (for any *Doctor Who* devotee) an instantly recognisable face was quite a surreal feeling, but it also gave me a real boost of confidence that I might be able to earn the trust of others by being so open about my own experiences.

The fact that Sophie was the only *Doctor Who* companion attending this event meant that I was meeting her almost by default, but after those few minutes in her company, I was really pleased that the companion I had met to tick off this challenge was Sophie Aldred.

It would be remiss of me not to mention all those who turned up to the event in various elaborate costumes – some of which I recognised, while others meant absolutely nothing at all. Apparently "cosplay" was all the rage – well, it wasn't in my house – and there was something inherently unnerving about nipping to the toilet and passing Patrick Troughton and an Imperial Stormtrooper on the way to the urinal!

Come to think of it, how *does* a Stormtrooper ...?

Actually, it's not really important.

As a brief aside, I later posted a copy of *Desperately Seeking Susan Foreman* to Judith Paris (who played the female version of Eldrad in a story called *The Hand of Fear*, which was the last classic adventure to feature the late Elisabeth Sladen as Sarah-Jane Smith). Judith had replied to a letter I had written to her with a signed photo and a note, explaining that her children both worked in the mental health sector, which gave a personal significance to the whole subject of raising awareness.

The book was sent by way of a thank you, and Judith actually telephoned to reciprocate those thanks when it arrived – such a nice gesture. Sadly, I was at work at the time, but Elaine was able to take the call, and said she was lovely ...

MEET A SECOND FORMER
DOCTOR WHO COMPANION

I also met another companion in 2015 (the challenge having reappeared on the second year's list). The event, Dimensions 2015, was also held in Newcastle, but this time the venue was the Copthorne Hotel.

It was a strange sort of a day, and I certainly learnt a lot about the nature of these clearly incredibly popular events and the apparent culture of what I believe is known as "fandom". The word I'd probably use to describe the overall experience would be (slightly) "uncomfortable".

Once again, there were a lot of people in costume (I still didn't see the attraction) but the most noticeable aspect of the day was that pretty much everything revolved around money. If you ignored the travel, accommodation, food, drink, etc., the price of admission was far from cheap (I had what amounted to the economy ticket ... and that cost £50). For that you were entitled to queue for an autograph from most of the guests, although there was a charge associated with others. But woe betide you if you asked for a photograph, because a series of separate "official" photoshoots would set you back anything from £15 to £40 ... each!

You could buy a silver or gold ticket that would gain you a number of "free" photos, but any extras meant another peek inside a wallet begging for mercy. On the basis that this "experience" was unlikely to ever be repeated, I had pre-ordered a photo with Daphne Ashbrook (who played Grace Holloway in the 1996 *Doctor Who* movie), and at the appointed time I joined the queue. It quickly grew into a very long queue, but happily I was about 10th in line ...

Well, I was – until gold pass holders were ushered to the front, with silver following right behind. As for me, with my contemptibly cheap £50 day pass and £15 photo ticket ...

'Please would you just join the back of the queue?'

The shoot itself was little more than a conveyor belt. Sit, smile, click, bye ... but now is the appropriate moment to mention the highlight of the day: meeting Daphne Ashbrook.

Daphne had been kind enough to send a lovely signed and dedicated photo all the way across the Atlantic for inclusion in *Desperately Seeking Susan Foreman*, and I was keen to give her a copy of the book and pass on my thanks in person.

A couple of hours before the official photo, I spent a couple of minutes in Daphne's company and explained about the book and my mental health awareness work. She was an absolute joy. I asked for the photo (to complete the challenge). She immediately agreed, although her "minder" was slightly more reluctant. The flash didn't go off, so the picture was a bit grainy, but it clearly showed a beaming former *Doctor Who* companion with her arms wrapped round me – I was clearly still very huggable.

I met three other people who had appeared in *Doctor Who* at various points during its near 52-year history, and I should also mention the lovely Jacqueline King, who played companion Donna Noble's mother Sylvia in relatively recent times. She took a real interest in what I had been doing, and the photo was absolutely no trouble at all.

From what I could gather, the level of interaction elsewhere very much depended on the allocated minder. One issued a refusal to a photo request that was blunt enough to actually take the actress concerned by surprise. Another looked like he was going to have palpitations when a former companion agreed to a quick photo that wasn't going to boost the coffers by that all-important £15 – cue a swift retraction.

It had been wonderful to meet Daphne and Jacqueline King. Despite the barriers, it was heart-warming to have such enthusiastic responses about mental health awareness.

CHAPTER 23

AFTER ALL THESE YEARS

I did wonder, when I decided to visit a few places that had some link to my past, whether I would somehow get a sense of having been there before – some meaningful feeling or a random memory. The "challenge" was obviously not the visit itself, but making contact with people I didn't know, talking to them about my mental health, explaining my connection with the place in question, and hoping some help might be forthcoming ...

Most of the locations were in York, the city where I was born and raised, but the quartet was completed by my hall of residence room at what had been the Polytechnic in Newcastle Upon Tyne.

VISIT MY FIRST HOME

Number 7, St Peter's Grove – in the Clifton area of York – was built towards the end of the 19th century, when it was home to a well-to-do Coney Street pharmacist named William Thompson, who lived with his family and five servants. By the time I entered the world in June 1964, however, the property had been acquired by St Peter's School as teacher accommodation and split into two flats, with the upper storey being renumbered 7a.

When Elaine and I arrived (in early 2014), it was clear to me that there had been massive changes over the preceding 50 years. The most obvious difference was that flats now stood on what had been our garden. I had spent so much time playing in what (through a child's eyes) was a massive expanse of grass, and I actually felt quite upset that so many memories had been covered by bricks and mortar.

That garden had witnessed countless games of football and cricket. There were great goals, brilliant spells of bowling and thrilling cover drives ... well, that's how I remembered them! There was a wall against which you could play "rebounds" with a football, play "catch" with a tennis ball, or practise your batting. On the other side of the wall was a densely tangled shrub that was able to take the weight of a child, and was therefore perfect for climbing. Another of the plants (near the steps to the door) had purple berries that looked like blood when you squeezed them, and every Sunday during the summer the ice-cream van pulled up just outside the gate. I would dash down the path to buy a double cone, one swirl of vanilla ice cream covered in chopped nuts, the other in chocolate sauce – all for six new pence!

The building itself was no longer flats. It was known as The Four Seasons Hotel, and had been owned and run by Steve and Bernice Roe for the previous 15 years or so. It was really nicely furnished and decorated, and I found it almost impossible to picture how it looked back in the mid-60s. Just as with the garden, what had been my bedroom also seemed so much smaller than I remembered, and even though the inside of the house bore very little resemblance to the place I called home all those years ago, it was still quite nice to think that I had spent some of my formative years in those very rooms. Sadly, though, I didn't get that feeling of having been there before.

The visit ended with an attempt to faithfully recreate a photograph taken around 1966, of me sitting on the steps outside the front door, reading a newspaper. Unfortunately, it had rained all morning ...

and we had forgotten to buy a newspaper ... and my dungaree shorts were still in the wash. So I adopted a casual crouching position for the picture and managed a nice smile, even though my knees were about to lock.

VISIT MY FIRST SCHOOL

By 1968 it was time to start school, and for the next four years I attended York College for Girls – a slight misnomer that was pretty much lost on my four-year-old self. In actual fact, it was the senior school that was girls only; boys were permitted (albeit heavily outnumbered) in the preparatory school.

In theoretic hindsight, I should have been spoilt for choice given the ratio of girls to boys, but back then I believed that not getting caught in a game of "kiss catch" was a smart thing to do. If I had my time again, I'd simply stand still, close my eyes, and shout, 'Take me!'

I hadn't set foot inside the imposing red building, which lay in the shadow of York Minster, for 45 years until April 2017, when I was offered the chance to be shown round by Lucienne (Lucy) Crux, who was a teacher at the Minster School, which had acquired the building after York College closed its doors for the final time in 1997.

I had a mental image of the interior (maintained by the number of times the school has featured in the vivid dreams I've had throughout my adult life), but I realised things would look very different in 2017 to how they had appeared to a child's eyes. Lucy and her mother (another former pupil) met me and Elaine outside the front door, but we strolled round to the back gates and entered the school via the playground.

The two giant concrete cylinders (used as playthings) were no longer there, and the outbuilding that used to store what we called "the apparatus" (it was like a big climbing frame) was now a music room.

The first port of call was the downstairs cloakroom, the ceiling of which, though I probably couldn't reach it when I was four, was now threating to inflict a serious head injury.

Upstairs to the early classrooms: Lower Preparatory, Upper Preparatory and Transition. I had clear memories of the last room. I could remember opening a door on the advent calendar and being able to choose whose turn it would be to open it the following day. I picked Sarah Wombell.

I always picked Sarah Wombell.

Miss Mason was my first teacher. The classroom was next to the foot of the main staircase. I recalled that there had been a large desk at the front of the room – and I had visions of collecting my latest Janet and John book from Miss Mason – and coloured blocks that we used to learn to count.

Up the main flight of stairs was the main hall, which seemed so tiny. It was used for assemblies as well as being the lunchtime dining area. The roast potatoes were amazing, but the rice pudding was revolting – and I haven't tried another spoonful to this day! You always longed for a slab of pure white Ebor ice cream, but equally you hoped that it didn't follow a particularly gristly piece of liver.

Just as with the look round my first home, this visit helped to bring back quite a few memories, but I didn't really get any real sense of connection. A pity, but it was still lovely to reminisce ...

RECEIVE A LETTER FROM A MEMBER OF THE ROYAL FAMILY

Coincidentally, that visit to my first school links directly into a challenge from 2014, one which involved me trying to obtain a letter from a member of the Royal Family. It looked a tough task on paper, but a rare piece of inspiration led to a wonderful response.

HRH The Duke of Kent,

ST. JAMES'S PALACE
LONDON SW1A 1BQ

4th April 2014

Dear Mr Kirby,

Thank you for your letter of 26th March, and for the photographs taken during my visit to York in the 1970's.

I was most interested to hear about the challenge you have set yourself in aid of the charity Mind for your fiftieth birthday, and I wish you every success in achieving the forty tasks on your list. Please accept this letter as completion of challenge No 18.

Yours sincerely,

Richard Kirby, Esq

My first attempt proved unsuccessful. I wrote to Prince Edward on the basis that we were born in the same year. He was due to turn 50 a couple of months before me, and I thought he'd jump at the chance to correspond with me.

I was mistaken.

And then I remembered I had not only met a member of the Royal Family – I actually had photographs to prove it!

The two pictures were taken in 1971 (not too long before my eighth birthday) when the Duke and Duchess of Kent paid a visit to York, 10 years after they married in York Minster. The photos seemed to suggest we had almost instantly built up a strong rapport, so armed with a couple of prints, I compiled my letter ...

By way of a little bit of background, Edward, Duke of Kent is a grandson of King George V. He was seventh in line to the throne when he was born in 1935. But following the birth of Zara Phillips' daughter Mia in 2014, Edward – who is the Queen's oldest living cousin – was 33rd in line of succession when I got in touch.

Princess Charlotte's arrival in 2015 knocked him one further place down the pecking order, but none of that mattered in the least when a typed, personally signed reply dropped through my letterbox.

The letter covers everything in just five lines – how you must be wishing I could have been so succinct!

BE PICTURED IN FRONT OF A FAMOUS NATIONAL LANDMARK

Taking the Royal theme one stage further, the 2017 challenge to be pictured outside a national landmark was fulfilled (several times over) during a short visit to London during April.

The landmark that officially ticked off the task was Buckingham Palace, the imposing and impressive structure that has been at the centre of so many memorable moments in this country's history – although it could just as easily have been Big Ben, Nelson's Column, Westminster Abbey, Kensington Palace etc.

Kensington Palace hosted an exhibition of dresses worn by Diana, Princess of Wales during the year that marked the 20th anniversary of her passing. Elaine was particularly keen to see not only the display, but also the newly opened (and beautiful) White Garden that had been created in Diana's memory.

We also had the chance to spend an evening with my elder daughter Leigh-Ann, who had lived and worked in the capital for a good few years. After a couple of drinks, we went for a meal to an Italian restaurant and, after perusing the menu, I picked the spicy pizza.

The waitress came to take our order, and to advise that pizzas were off the menu. You can imagine my disappointment – and the waitress kindly said she would pop into the kitchen, have a quick chat with the chef, and see what she could do. A few minutes later, she bounded back to our table with a huge grin on her face, offered her hand for me to 'high five' and excitedly announced that they could accommodate one more pizza. What would I like to order …?

'I'll have the risotto.'

Well, I thought it was funny.

VISIT MY HALLS OF RESIDENCE ROOM FROM 1982–83

And now from one of the most lavish buildings in the land to one small room in a hall of residence that I called home between October 1982 and the summer of 1983.

Now the University of Northumbria, it was just plain old Newcastle Upon Tyne Polytechnic back then, and my room was number 9 in the Monkchester East Hall on the Coach Lane campus, situated a few miles (or a few Metro stops) away from the city centre.

Although I was only there for nine short months – an insignificant period given my age – my time at Coach Lane had a lasting impact on me.

I was an immature and naive 18-year-old who wasn't really prepared for student life. It took me several weeks to settle into my new surroundings and begin to properly integrate. I had never had to fend for myself, and I soon learnt that I was as bad at cooking and washing as I was at managing money.

Obviously, the main reason I was there was to study, but I'll never fully understand why the course I chose comprised French, German, politics and economics. I was a reasonably good linguist, but had very little interest in politics, and absolutely none at all in economics. I had zero ability in the latter as well, so as far as first year exams were concerned. The writing was on the proverbial wall from an early stage in proceedings.

(As it turned out, the economics paper was the only one out of 12 that I failed – but I failed it by a distance, and with that I was forced to bid farewell to further education.)

From an emotional perspective, it was certainly an intense time. Being on my own in a relatively small room, with just my collection of tapes and vinyl 45s for company, offered far too much time for reflection and introspection, and there were periods when I felt incredibly low – and lonely. That said, company was never far away and, over time, I made some good mates, most notably my Rush and Toto-playing neighbour Stephen.

I did have a couple of close friendships, both of which were important to me. One was destined to end in tears (all of which were mine) as the girl concerned already had – and ultimately kept – a boyfriend. The other was with Ruth, with whom I got on really well. We went out, she dumped me ... twice.

But I'm not bitter.

In fact, our paths crossed – albeit virtually – a few years ago (via a Valentine's Day blog of all things), and it has been lovely to be back in touch.

My overriding feeling about that year away was that it was something of an unfinished chapter in my life. I realise that might sound strange, given that I'm going back more than three decades. And it's also really hard to try to explain, but some of the memories (both good and bad) are still incredibly strong, and somehow become more vivid at certain times of the year.

Perhaps I had never fully come to terms with my abiding sense of failure, I honestly don't know, but those months at Coach Lane had such a profound effect on me that parts of the campus (as I remembered them) formed the setting for my debut novel.

I wanted to see my old room to give me some sort of closure – if that's the right word.

Anyway, back to 2014, and it was pretty miserable when I arrived. I was met by the Project Officer Gary Wilson. He explained that all the old buildings on the far side of the campus that had formerly been halls of residence now lay empty, in varying states of (dis)repair, waiting to be sold off as a housing development.

Until relatively recently, I had no photographs at all from my year at Coach Lane (and even now I only have one). However, on approaching Monkchester East Hall, despite the overgrown grass and hedges, the building itself looked the same as I remembered it.

Gary unlocked the outer door and there, on the left as I faced along the short corridor, was room number 9.

In reality, all I was about to do was enter an empty room. But it was the weirdest feeling ...

It seemed small. The cupboard, shelving and sink (aka unofficial toilet) were probably just as they'd been back in 1982. In my mind, the bed (complete with green blanket), table, chair and rug all reappeared. The side wall was once again decorated with old York City football programmes, and another punk single (purchased from my unauthorised overdraft) span on the turntable, just waiting for the needle to be lowered.

Surreal ... but briefly wonderful.

The shared toilet and bathroom were still directly opposite my room, with bedrooms once occupied by Brian, Stephen and Paul leading to the kitchen. The food lockers were empty but ready to be padlocked. If only I'd brought some white bread and cheddar spread with me ...

I must be honest (and without wanting to be unnecessarily overdramatic), it took some time to get my head around the strength of feelings and emotions brought back by those few minutes. Even now, I'm still not sure if I got the closure I felt I needed, but having the chance to visit that room one last time was massively important to me, and I hope I've managed to convey some sense of what the experience was like.

RECREATE A FAVOURITE TEENAGE PHOTOGRAPH

In order to do this photographic challenge, I had to return to the place I had called home for the majority of the 1970s through to the mid-80s – and, for most of that period, it had been my school as well.

My father was a teacher at St Peter's School in York for nearly 40 years; he also ran a boarding house called The Rise. The task in question was to recreate a favourite photo from yesteryear, and the picture in question featured me and my mother, Anna, sitting on the steps of The Rise – probably not long after my return from college.

In 2016, St Peter's School was far removed from the establishment where I grew up. I now needed a visitor's pass to walk around the place where I spent so much of my young life. Most areas of the school were secured by key-code-operated gates and locks, and a number of the buildings I remembered had been replaced by 21st century equivalents.

I kept thinking back to "my day", when things almost by definition were far better. But in reality, my memories were just a snapshot of a time that would soon be all but forgotten by inevitable progress. Perhaps that was no bad thing, given how hard it actually was to grow up in such an unusual environment.

But strolling through the grounds with Mum and Elaine wasn't the time to dwell on the less pleasant moments and feelings that remained so fresh in my mind despite the intervening decades. The visit was a chance to remember how things used to look, not necessarily how they used to be: the long since demolished air raid shelter, the huts that had been the junior school classrooms, the conker trees that were felled to make way for the sports centre – I'd wager very few remember those. There was the area where we played marbles ('Hit one, win the lot … your hard luck if it doesn't reach'), Mrs Wrigley's tuck shop, the squash court and maintenance workshops that were situated where the new science block now stood …

Now for the photograph …

Mother and son – then and now.

Well, it wasn't a faithful recreation, as the heavens chose the worst possible moment to open, and Mum and I had to assume the 32-year-old pose while sitting on a jacket instead of a sun-soaked step. We still managed to smile through the downpour.

What the pictures clearly showed was that Mum still looked amazing at 78.

Me?

I got old!

CHAPTER 24

THE HEALING POWER
OF SPORT

During the 1990s and into the new millennium, I was a keen, albeit slow, jogger. The main reason for pounding the streets in and around Gateshead (where I lived at the time) was to maintain a reasonable level of fitness for the sports that I played and enjoyed – namely cricket and badminton.

But there was an added benefit, in that running actually seemed to clear my head. Whether I'd had a crap day at work, or was generally just feeling below par, then anything from a 3-mile to a 10-mile run would almost always lighten my mood.

In fairness, however, I could hardly say the benefits were immediate. The first time I plucked up the courage to go for a jog (one cold and thankfully dark October evening in 1992), I lasted all of a quarter of a mile before my chest began to burn and I couldn't catch my breath. Not the most auspicious of starts, but I decided to try again a couple of days later, and over the weeks that followed, I managed to complete a mile ... then 2 miles ... then 3 ...

If I left my house and turned right onto the main road, the run to the iconic Angel of the North and back was roughly one and three-quarter miles. Turn left, and there was a three-and-a-quarter-mile circuit down to the bridge near the old Swallow Hotel in Gateshead. Add the two together, you had a five-mile run. Longer distances could be reasonably accurately calculated using combinations of these two routes.

The shorter runs tended to be against the clock – with the achievement of a personal best occasionally and frustratingly being determined by the vagaries of traffic light sequences. I would normally run my longer distances – anything longer than 6 miles – on a Sunday morning. The roads would usually be fairly quiet, and that gave me the perfect opportunity to reflect. My train of thought was far less likely to be interrupted by yet another line of turning cars.

Jogging for anything between one and two hours in the fresh morning air, with all the sights and sounds of people simply going about their lives, was so enjoyable. Running rarely failed to give me some respite from my worries and issues. Physically I felt really strong, and I'm sure that helped my emotional wellbeing as well.

I continued to train after the cricket season had started, because I'd managed to get a place in the 1993 Great North Run. A few months earlier, that wheezing wreck could not have imagined attempting a half-marathon, but I did complete the 13-mile course not once, but five times. Each was an amazing experience. My average time was around two and a half hours – by no means quick, but entering the race was an expensive business and it was important to get value for money!

Running had helped me in so many ways. If some new-found self-belief was the cake, the icing on the top came from the sense of achievement I got each time I crossed the finish line in South Shields.

Unfortunately, I started to suffer more and more problems with my knees (the right one in particular), and it reached the stage when my right leg would often simply give way when I was out running. I'd had scans; the joint was stable, but the pain kept increasing to the point when I could barely get up and down a flight of stairs.

That was when I was diagnosed with my chronic hip problem. Eventually a scan on my hips revealed the root cause of what had been referred pain. It brought an immediate end to my jogging exploits. It also forced me to retire from cricket (some would say I never actually started) and stop my weekly games of badminton because my hips were deteriorating to the extent that I'd need both replacing within a couple of years if I carried on.

Not surprisingly I did as I was told, although it was incredibly tough realising that I would never again be smashed out of a cricket ground or stand by and watch shuttlecocks whizzing past my racket.

The reality hit me really hard, but over time I learnt to manage the condition well – to the extent that I was able to include some physical activities within the challenges.

It wasn't until 2016 that I discovered that sessions on an indoor rowing machine gave me a boost that was similar to how I used to feel after a run. Obviously given that the machine is stationary, you don't get the fresh air or changes in scenery, but the element of distraction is now provided by the ridiculously loud music being fed into my one good ear through a pleasantly inexpensive set of headphones.

Just as with those Great North Runs, there is a definite feeling of accomplishment you get from rowing – and that accompanies the physical and mental benefits. And as far as my hips are concerned, the low-impact nature of the repetitive movement hopefully means I will be able to carry on rowing for many years to come.

I was never particularly good at chemistry or physics when I was at school, but even with my limited knowledge, I still realised there had to be some scientific reason for the "feel good factor" that exercise gave me. It seemed clear that any explanation might include the brain chemical serotonin, which is reasonably well known for regulating and having a positive influence on things such as sleep patterns, emotion and mood.

And lo and behold ...

Serotonin is a monoamine neurotransmitter (trust me …). Essentially, it's a chemical messenger that carries signals between nerve cells in the brain. Although many neurotransmitters work together to influence mood (dopamine being one example), serotonin is seemingly one of the most important. High levels of serotonin in the brain are associated with elevated mood and vice versa. Serotonin production can be stimulated by diet, sunlight and … exercise.

I did research the ways in which physical activity increases serotonin in the brain, but it was getting to the stage where I was looking up the meaning of every second or third word, so I'm hoping you'll just take it as read that especially aerobic exercise can really enhance mood through increasing brain serotonin levels.

As a brief aside, it is also possible to enhance serotonin levels through taking certain medication. After carrying a message, serotonin is usually reabsorbed by the nerve cells (the technical term is "reuptake"). This means that more serotonin is then required to pass further messages between nerve cells. But depression medications known as Selective Serotonin Reuptake Inhibitors (SSRIs) have the ability to block (i.e. "inhibit") reuptake, thereby meaning there is more serotonin available.

Depression, in whatever form, is not simply caused by low serotonin levels, and SSRIs can cause a number of possible side effects. So, they are far from a cure-all, but in some cases heightened serotonin levels can have a positive effect on symptoms.

No two people and no two mental health diagnoses are exactly the same, and those differences will also apply to the level of response to various types of treatment.

Despite this, there seems to be strong medical evidence that exercise can improve your wellbeing. It has certainly made a positive difference to me.

CHAPTER 25

MORE THAN A PHELAN

I'm not sure quite where I got my love of writing. I always enjoyed languages (hence why I did French, German and Latin at A level), but I continually struggled with literature. As a youngster, I loved reading anything to do with facts and figures, but reading fictional prose was (and remains) a bit of a chore for me.

I compiled fanzines for Gateshead Football Club and then Gateshead Thunder (rugby league) during the mid- to late-90s and into the new millennium. I really wanted to try to write a "proper" book, but the opportunity never really arose until after I'd finished playing cricket.

Since Elaine and I got together in 2006, I have written a number of non-fiction works covering subjects such as Hollywood actresses (Marilyn Monroe, Marie Prevost, and my absolute movie idol Jean Harlow), the American astronaut Virgil "Gus" Grissom, the Wineville Chicken Murders (that were adapted into the Angelina Jolie film *Changeling*), rugby league, and of course *Doctor Who* – the last-named leading to a publishing contract and fulfilment of a dream.

Back in 2004, however, shortly after a revelation that completely changed the course of my life, I started to write a novel.

COMPLETE THE NOVEL I STARTED IN 2004

Over the years that followed I wrote, changed, deleted, wrote again ... and again. A decade after typing those first words I finally completed the book – and a 2014 challenge in the process.

The book is called *The Beige Beetle* and this is the synopsis:

Matthew Green was 18 and just starting his first year as a university student. He hoped that being away from home might help him finally come to terms with certain events from his past, but his demons refused to release their grip – until a chance meeting that would have the most dramatic effect on not one, but two lives.

The book was so difficult to write, and the main reason why I found the process so challenging was the fact that parts of Matthew's character and some of his experiences were based on me and my life. Interspersed within those real-life elements is a sizeable proportion of pure fiction, and no one will ever fully know which bits are true and which I simply made up.

I began to react really badly when I tried to recall emotive memories from the past, but in a sense it was still easier to remember things that had actually happened rather than creating scenarios, events and associated feelings. I wanted to allow the story to develop naturally and ensure that Matthew grew into a rounded and credible character.

Whenever the burden of reliving the past got too much, I had to stop writing to allow the negativity to subside. But then I would lose my train of thought and I always struggled to pick up the thread and pace of the story. Basically, the dilemma was that I needed to be "in character" to produce (what I considered to be) my best work, but that being the case, it was only ever a matter of time before it became harder and harder to think clearly and the pressure would quickly build to a point where I could no longer continue.

I then had to introduce Jodie and try to give the reader an understanding of her own issues – which was hard, because I didn't fully understand them myself at the start. Then there was the relationship between the pair to consider, as well as the beginning and ending.

But there was one positive – opening up about my dysthymia was something of a release, and in a similar way so was writing about aspects of my own personality. It allowed me to unburden myself, at least before things got too heavy. I think it helped that I had the relative safety of hiding behind an outwardly fictional character.

I'm honestly not sure if I would ever have finished the novel had I not effectively forced my own hand by including it in list of challenges. But it was a book that needed to be written, and needed to be finished. I am incredibly proud of *The Beige Beetle*.

Obviously, I never thought for a moment that the book would bring me fame and fortune. To be honest, I'm not greedy – I'd have settled for just the fortune. But I always genuinely believed that the story was worth reading. I was equally interested to learn what other people (especially those who were regular readers) thought about the book. The first person prepared to commit thoughts to (electronic) paper and critique *The Beige Beetle* was Sarah Corden-Lloyd (a former classmate who I met up with again). Sarah promised to be honest, which worried me, but here is her appraisal of my novel:

I really enjoyed the book, Richard – I think you write beautifully and the characters are totally believable. I was interested in them both and their lives. And, of course, it was clever of you to provide tension right from the beginning – it meant I couldn't wait to get to the end!

Very very good insight into the female mind. Conversation was well thought through and easy to read – and yes, I liked the plot and [spoiler alert] the fact it wasn't a happy ending. It left me wanting more.

I suppose the only thing I would say is that although I was sympathetic toward the couple, I felt a little too sorry for them, but that is such a minor observation. Really, I was hugely impressed!

Clearly, you're now intrigued and eager, verging on impatient to settle down and read the book. Therefore, as part of the appetite-whetting process, here is an extract from Chapter 3 – the moment when the two main characters speak to each other properly for the first time:

The measure of my lack of preparation for the hours ahead lay in the fact that I actually considered spending a bit of time on an essay that wasn't even nearly due for completion. Whatever happened to last minute?

I got as far as leaning across the desk to grab the half-used pad of A4 paper, but before I had the chance to choose from my assortment of biros – all with chewed tops – there was a gentle tap at the door. Given my fairly reclusive existence, I wasn't usually inundated with visitors, but what was intriguing was not so much the fact that someone was outside my room, but that the sound of the knock was so soft it was barely audible. I dropped the paper onto my desk, crossed the room and opened the door. My heart actually skipped a beat when I realised it was Jodie – a tell-tale, albeit totally unexpected reaction which caused me to inhale sharply. We'd chatted quite a few times since that initial, rather surreal, meeting. The exchanges had been brief, stilted, but important to me at least, because I was really attracted to her.

Jodie didn't notice. She was gazing down towards the floor, but as she raised her head it was pretty obvious she'd been crying.

'Are you okay?'

Jodie smiled – weakly.

'I was just wondering if you knew where Phil was?'

Phil occupied the room next door to me, at the very end of the corridor. I'd not spent a great deal of time in his company, but he was loud and his attempts at humour were both near the proverbial knuckle and unfunny in equal measure. I can't quite describe his voice (although it did have a distinctive West Yorkshire twang), except to say that he spoke on a frequency that you couldn't escape. Even in a crowded room, his voice seemed to scythe through any level of general buzz, and he clearly relished his self-appointed life and soul status.

'Sorry, no. Are ... are you okay?'

Jodie attempted a smile. 'I'm fine Matt, thanks.' She then seemed to hesitate – I don't know who she was trying to convince, but she looked so pale and fragile, something had clearly upset her. 'Actually, I'm not really okay. Do you mind, if I, er, come in for a minute?'

'Yeah. Of course. Here ...' I held the door open and Jodie shuffled in.

The door had one of those mechanisms that made it shut automatically, but for some reason, my door seemed to have a mind of its own. Normally it would close slowly, almost serenely, but without the force to shut completely, but if you ever left the room without your key – which I had managed twice in a matter of weeks – then the bloody thing flew back and slammed shut with a thud that was instantly followed by a string of well-chosen expletives.

Jodie sat on the edge of the bed – right on the edge. I plumped for the opposite end of the bed (the pillow end) and almost wedged myself into the corner of the room, trying, but probably failing, to appear relaxed – because having an attractive girl sitting on my bed was the most natural thing in the world ...

Which it wasn't ...

Anyway, after a silence that probably lasted no more than a couple of seconds, but felt more like a minute, Jodie whispered: 'I'm sorry Matt, this isn't really fair. I didn't mean to bother you.'

'It's fine,' I replied in my best upbeat voice. 'Is there anything I can do?'

Jodie took a deep breath, straightened her back and flicked a hand across the side of her face, brushing some hair behind her left ear: 'I ... I just wanted to talk to someone.'

'You can talk to me if you want,' was more of a plea than a reply.

'Really?'

'Well yeah – but only if I'm not getting in the way?'

'Phil?'

I nodded.

'No, it's nothing like that.'

Jodie suddenly seemed much more composed and assured. Although we were sitting several feet apart, she moved slightly – which was a relief because she'd been pretty precariously balanced on the edge of the bed – and leant towards me: 'Well, I've just got one lecture this morning, so if you're free later, we could go for a coffee?'

'What about the Green Dragon? They do hot drinks, but we could have something a bit stronger if you wanted?'

'That would be great!'

'Is twelve okay?'

'Perfect. And thank you!'

'It's really fine – I could do with some company too.'

Jodie glanced at me out of the corner of her eyes: 'Really? Is everything okay with you, Matt?'

'Yeah,' I fibbed. But it was a convincing fib. 'I'll see you at twelve. Just meet you there, yeah?'

'See you there!' Jodie jumped to her feet and opened the door, flashing a smile as she left that caused my chest to instantly tighten.

As I heard the main outer door click shut, my brain finally lost control of a right hand that had been desperate to make a fist and punch the air. I was tempted to go over to the window and watch Jodie on her way back to her own Hall. "Watch" would be a bit of an exaggeration really, because the buildings were situated quite close together and there was only a small bit of the main path through the campus that was visible from my room.

On the other hand, if I caught just the tiniest glimpse of her, then it would make what had just happened undeniably real – and at that moment, it didn't feel real at all. Yet there I was, sitting quite still, gazing blankly (it was an expression that came naturally) at the opposite wall, as the realisation dawned that Jodie and I would be sharing a drink in just a couple of hours.

My mind was racing now though – partly out of curiosity as to what Jodie wanted to talk about and (even though I wasn't her first choice) why she was willing to talk to me – but also there was a feeling of anticipation that I'd maybe get the chance to reveal how low I'd been feeling. Or was that a bit selfish?

I suppose much depended on what Jodie was going to say – so why didn't I just bloody stop thinking and just wait and see? If only it were that easy – after all, thinking was the thing I did best ...

BE PICTURED OUTSIDE THE ROVERS RETURN

Now we move from a fictional book to a fictional television series. On a damp Manchester afternoon in May 2014, I stood outside the Rovers Return (a pub in *Coronation Street*) and, in doing so, ticked off another task.

Elaine and I had been on a tour round the old Granada studios, we'd sat in the Green Room, peered into various dressing rooms, seen some of the internal sets, sat in the Rovers Return (complete with absolutely brand-new dartboard) and listened to the guide talk to us as if we were seven!

We even got to stand behind the bar, home to so many iconic figures from Annie and Jack Walker right through to the 2014 incumbents Steve McDonald and Michelle Connor. I could have sat and reminisced for hours, but studio tours wait for no man!

Coronation Street is no longer the gritty tale of northern folk. Now it's a main competitor in a ratings war that demands storylines which can sometimes captivate a nation, but also stretch even the most vivid imagination. As we strolled down the Weatherfield cobbles, we realised that practically every house we passed would – at some point or another – have witnessed deaths, disasters, serious crimes (the number of which will be way above the statistical average for one street), tears of joy and sadness, champagne comedy moments, and a million other memories.

The set had undergone many changes during the previous five decades, and as much as it was hard to believe, there we were walking the same path as Elsie Tanner, Stan and Hilda, Jack and Vera et al., and sitting in the same pub as the likes of Ena, Minnie and Martha. The fact that being pictured outside the Rovers Return was one of my challenges was arguably incidental – we had been surrounded by television history, and had enjoyed an hour or so of self-indulgent soap magic!

MEET AN ACTOR WHO HAS APPEARED IN *CORONATION STREET*

If I thought Corrie-related challenges couldn't get any better, I would be proved totally wrong in July 2017, when Elaine and I were invited to the actual real working set … and had the chance to meet a member of the current cast!

For me, this particular task clearly demonstrated that you never know quite where you might end up if you're prepared to talk and ask for help. In a mental health context, you might be supported to take the first steps on a path towards recovery – but in this particular case the steps in question were on probably the most famous cobbles in the world.

At the time I was in reasonably regular contact with Michelle Holmes, who had played barmaid Tina Fowler in *Corrie* back in the late 80s. She had been so supportive when we'd first spoken back in

With Elaine and Connor McIntyre on the Weatherfield cobbles.

2012, and it was nice to share news via an occasional email over the years that followed. And then, in the summer of 2017, I messaged her telling her about my recently completed and remaining challenges.

Michelle replied that she'd been in touch with a friend who worked in the programme's casting department to see if it might be possible to arrange a visit – and help me tick off a task that I was seriously considering moving to the file marked "forlorn hope". It was a remarkably generous gesture from someone I had still not actually met ...

Literally minutes later, Michelle sent another message with an email address for Joanne Moss, who worked on the show. I wrote to Joanne and, within a few days, we agreed on a date and time for me and Elaine to go to the *Coronation Street* studios (on Salford Quays in Manchester)!

Apart from our respective work managers, virtually no one knew about the trip. We genuinely had no idea what to expect, and I certainly didn't want to tempt fate by giving the day the big build-up. We gave ourselves plenty of time to get to Manchester, but the journey was pleasantly uneventful and we arrived at the studio gates just after midday.

There were half a dozen people waiting outside the gates, clearly in the hope of getting an autograph or photo from one of the cast as they drove into or out of the site. It felt a bit weird – almost uncomfortable – but I suppose that's partly because the only person who had ever waited any length of time for me to appear was a bailiff ...

The security guards (of which there were several) directed me to a parking spot, at which point Elaine exclaimed, 'There's Norris!'

And sure enough, it was Norris – or rather actor Malcolm Hebden – just popping out for what I believe is known as a "fag break" and a chat with Dolly-Rose Campbell (who plays Gemma). We went to reception, signed in and got our visitors' badges. While we were waiting for Joanne, a smiling Catherine Tyldesley (Eva) walked past us, out of the building and back to her car!

Joanne appeared soon after, and the conversation flowed right from the moment we introduced ourselves. We walked into a rest area, and I held the door open for an attractive young lady in a flowing flowery dress.

'Thank you very much,' she said, at which point I realised it was Georgia Taylor (Toyah), who (as we soon discovered) was actually on her way for a photoshoot – all very surreal.

Joanne explained that for the actors, the studio complex was their "safe haven", and it was important that they could go about their work without constant requests for autographs and pictures, which would evidently start literally from the moment the exit barrier was raised. They are some of the most recognisable faces on our television screens, but there are real people behind the characters and knowing the character is not the same as knowing the actual person.

We were well aware what a privilege it was simply to be there – reaffirmed by the fact there aren't even official tours – and it was only right to respect the privacy of those cast members who were basically just doing their job.

However, the situation was different if a particular actor knew that someone was coming to see them, and Joanne then revealed that she'd set up a meeting with Connor McIntyre, who plays the resident villain Pat Phelan.

Joanne said he was a lovely man, with a real interest in what I'd been doing.

Wow!

Joanne escorted us to the external set and showed us inside some of the shops (shattering a number of illusions in the process). Georgia was being photographed outside the Rovers Return, but after she'd moved to another part of the set, it was our turn to be pictured in front of the iconic public house.

Interesting fact: this Rovers Return has two front bedroom windows, but the pub in the old set (which we'd visited in 2014) only had one.

From there we went into Studio 2, which contained some of the internal sets including Roy's Rolls – complete with worryingly realistic fake sandwiches – and the front room of Dev's house. Joanne explained so much about the difficulties of continuity, particularly when scenes were shot out of sequence (for example hair length and colour, or a tan gained from a brief holiday, even the dates of magazines and how they're arranged on a table.) All logical, I suppose, but it was fascinating to hear how even the smallest detail was important.

Soon after, we were led into the canteen and Connor arrived.

Interesting fact number two: Connor was born just a few days before the first ever episode of *Coronation Street* was transmitted.

It's quite hard to describe what it's like to leave your house and, four hours and 120 miles later, be sitting talking with a *Coronation Street* actor. But I have to say it felt far more natural than I could have imagined. It helped that Connor was wonderful and engaging company. He asked me about my reasons for doing the challenges, and we chatted about one or two individual tasks.

Connor made sure everyone was part of the conversation. I could see that Elaine was enjoying every moment, and seeing her so happy just made the day even more special. We headed outside for a few photographs, including a couple on the main set with The Kabin and Dev's shop in the background, before it was time for Connor to get back to work.

We'd loved meeting Joanne and Connor, as well as seeing several other Weatherfield residents – we also spotted Richard Hawley (Johnny), Harry Visinoni (Seb) and Nicola Thorp (Nicola) – but eventually, after two magical hours, it was time to get back into the car and drive slowly back into the real world ...

CHAPTER 26

DEAR RICHARD

Dear Young Richard

It is something like 46 years ago that I stood in the garden, looking very smart in my school uniform, and almost smiled for Mum's instamatic camera.

I know you can't wait to change into your football kit, get back into the garden and score a few more goals. But as the older man who one day you'll grow to become, I have this chance to write you a letter. One day I hope you'll get the opportunity to read it.

Right now, your life is nice and straightforward. You go to school, come home, have tea, go out and play. Mum and Dad are there, as is your sister. Nannie and Grandad and Gran and Grandad are in Croft and Darlington, and everything is good. You know this.

But when you are 12, your grandad (Eric) will pass away. You'll be too young to fully understand, but the memory of the day will never leave you. Gran, Grandad Les and Nannie are all gone now, in my time. You will miss them so much – and it's fine to miss them – but even though they knew how much you loved them, you will feel guilty for not telling them.

Make sure you enjoy every minute with them.

Just one word of warning, though – don't ever think you can beat Nannie at cards. She's way too good, and the more you lose, the more she'll laugh!

Mum and Dad are still here. They're nearly 80 now ... I know ... really old ... but they are amazing. There will be times when you don't think you need them, but they'll always be there for you and never give up on you when you get things wrong. And I mean badly wrong.

You will grow up to have some good qualities. You will be caring, kind, loyal and trusting ... too trusting at times. You will make mistakes, some that will completely change the course of your life. But believe me, Richard, you will find you have the inner resolve to fight so hard, and you will get there in the end.

Eventually.

You will be there to see the birth of two daughters. Right now, you can't imagine anything better than scoring a winning goal for York City, but hormones and all that. Things won't always run smoothly – and yes, some of that will be your fault, but you will also burden yourself with guilt that is not yours to carry. The truth will come out, and when it does, remember your children are what matter. Just be there, be strong, be honest: things will work out, I promise.

You will try your hand at a few jobs. You'll work in shops and offices, but when the chance comes to work in the NHS, grab it with both hands because you will meet the woman who will make you truly happy. Just so you don't pick the wrong one, she's called Elaine – her life has had its ups and downs too, but you are perfect for each other.

All I will say is that the best things in life are worth fighting for, so don't you dare give up. You will wish you'd met when you were teenagers, but fate could have easily made sure your paths never crossed. Love her always, Richard – she's the one ...

I'm happy to say you will play lots of cricket. You're not brilliant, but you're not bad. Make the most of every moment, because your joints will pack up when you're 40 and then there'll be a big void in your life.

You'll try lots of other sports – you'll be quite good at some – but sadly football won't be one of them! You'll even take up long-distance running when you're 30. I know that right now you think you can sprint like Valeriy Borzov, but sadly the Richard writing this letter can barely run like Valerie Singleton.

One big surprise is that you will become a published author ... who'd have thought! And even when people say how much they enjoy your books, you will still doubt yourself. But you can write – and you can be quite funny at times too.

You got that from me!

It's nearly time for me to go now, Richard, but before I do, I've got two bits of advice for you: firstly, stay true to yourself. You won't be perfect – far from it. And some of your better qualities will also be your weaknesses. But as well as a brilliant wife, you will also have a few friends who make a real difference – just keep believing in yourself, because you make a difference too.

Oh, and secondly, go to the bookies in August 1983 and put all your money on York City to win the 4th division title. They win it by a mile and you'll be loaded!

Be happy ... and try not to worry ... you'll be absolutely fine.

Lots of love,

Big Richard x

CHAPTER 27

TIME TO TALK

HAVE AN ARTICLE PRINTED IN A NEWSPAPER

Another challenge I based around writing was to have an article printed in a newspaper. This actually happened twice during 2014; the first being a full-page feature about my challenges in *The Canarian Weekly*, the Canary Islands' only English paper. Here is part of it:

The first question I get asked about the 40Fifty Challenge I've set myself for the year of my 50th birthday is this: 'Why are there 40 challenges and not 50?'

The official answer is that I wanted to recognise how much my life has changed since I turned 40 – the real reason is I ran out of ideas! That said, I have compiled a list of pretty random tasks – some, on the face of it, relatively easy and others less so. But I hope they'll be interesting and diverse enough to create some interest, and ultimately help me to raise some money for the mental health charity Mind.

So while I will hopefully bowl at a county cricketer, visit a television studio, sell a picture that I've drawn (I can't draw), have a photograph taken with a London 2012 medallist, have a bird of prey fly onto my hand, attempt the hottest curry on an Indian restaurant menu, shave my head, track down a classmate from my first school, play goal shooter in a netball team, bid at an auction and hold a snake (a real one, I hasten to add) and more besides, I do not wish to lose sight of the charitable cause.

A number of years ago I was diagnosed with a form of depression: unseen, but so horribly debilitating. I'd outwardly cope with life's ups and downs because ... well, because isn't that what everybody does? And I'd try so hard to hide the occasional irrational thoughts, but there comes a point when it just gets too much.

This is basically what happened back in 2011. It resulted in two incredibly difficult yet significant moments. The first was to sit down in front of the team I managed at work and explain I was suffering from depression. I was encouraged not to do it because it was so personal, but I just had to – and given their response to hearing me speak so openly, I'm so glad I did.

The second was to post a blog about my experiences, written in the aftermath of the tragic suicide of Gary Speed. I didn't want sympathy; I just wanted to tell my story. The reaction from family and friends was so positive, and I know I am incredibly lucky to be married to Elaine, whose love and support during the occasional dark times has been wonderful beyond words.

In the scheme of things, I'm nobody important – but in a sense, that's just the point. Sufferers from mental illness in whatever form can come from any background, any walk of life: even the strongest aren't immune. But standing up and asking for help is not a sign of weakness – in actual fact, acceptance is the first, hardest and bravest step on the road that will hopefully lead towards recovery. I might not make much of a difference, but one thing's for sure: if I do nothing, then I'll make absolutely no difference at all.

I wrote the majority of the article myself, but getting it printed was very much down to the influence of Maggie Lennard, who was (at the time) living in Tenerife. She was working for a local radio station and had strong media contacts on the island. Maggie got in touch to let me know she might be able to help, and just a couple of days later she messaged again to tell me I'd better start typing! I've since met up with Maggie twice over the past five or six years, although we hadn't seen each other for probably in excess of a quarter of a century before then. For the record, as well as being a long-standing friend, Maggie is also my elder daughter Leigh-Ann's godmother.

After playing club cricket for so many years, there had been a few occasions when I'd sneaked into a press report. There were even a couple of "action shots" of me that surfaced from time to time, so seeing my name in print wasn't a new experience. I could almost cope with my face gazing back at me, but the big difference was the subject matter of the article.

There is a huge jump from taking a couple of wickets on a Saturday afternoon to revealing you have a mental health condition. But (much as with that first live radio interview) I needed to focus on the importance of the story, rather than get greatly distracted or emotionally preoccupied with the reaction of my unseen audience.

The second newspaper appearance was much closer to home – a further lengthy article in our local daily, *The Evening Gazette*.

The feature was on page seven. If I remember correctly, *The Daily Star* used to include a 'page seven fella' many moons ago, presumably as some sort of contrast to a tabloid rival's universally known topless page three models. It was comforting to know that Teesside's daily paper was continuing the tradition of hunky men appearing on this particular page ...

This time I wasn't directly responsible for the content, and the opening paragraph certainly gave me the big build-up. It stated that I was "brave" (I'm not) and that the challenge was "taking the country by storm" (it was barely taking my house by storm).

Obviously, I wasn't naive enough to expect my words to be quoted verbatim, and the article did employ an element of journalistic licence to overstate a few things – for instance, I might have had some difficult times in my life, but I wouldn't have called it "a troubled past", and my hip condition didn't mean that I couldn't run. It just bloody hurt if I tried.

No matter … all publicity, as they say!

COMPILE A BLOG ABOUT MY MENTAL HEALTH EXPERIENCES FOR TIME TO CHANGE

After working with the charity Mind in 2014, I began my association with their Time to Change movement the following year, during which I registered as a "champion" (as in the Wonder Horse). My first involvement with the programme was to write a blog for their website, in which I tried to explain the effects of my condition, how it made me feel and how much stronger I had ultimately become.

Much of the content appears in various guises within these pages, so there is no need to reproduce the blog here, but the article did elicit a few replies and comments, and this was one:

Richard, your story really did strike me in a way that other pieces of writing haven't before.

It describes so much for me in terms of being told it would be best if I see a doctor even though I was scared to. It took a year until I eventually sought help. I remember how I felt in that doctor's visit … getting upset when speaking to my GP.

My family didn't know anything about my depression until I had to be forced to tell them. I tried counselling, but it didn't work for me. I'm now on antidepressants and they are working, as they're helping me fight back and giving me a way of coping with these feelings I'm experiencing. They also help me help myself a little bit more. This story brings me hope that I can still have a life and depression doesn't have to control me. I do still struggle but I'm finding a way to live my life. Lots of love, Dionne x

I didn't know anything about Dionne, but to have perhaps made a small difference to a total stranger meant such a lot and justified everything about talking so openly and honestly about a subject some would still prefer to avoid.

ORGANISE A "TIME TO TALK" EVENT

In an earlier chapter, I included an article in which I tried to explain how my symptoms actually made me feel. That formed the basis for a Time to Change work event in 2016, where I invited anyone who was interested to come along and ask me pretty much anything about my condition (with cake used as an enticement).

About a dozen colleagues came along (it was good cake) and the hour that followed was intense, difficult, draining, yet hugely rewarding. I did my best to answer the questions as honestly as I could, but after maybe half an hour or so, I became aware that I was only making eye contact with the table. I never felt like I was being judged, but equally I'd never spoken at such length about the reality and day-to-day effects of dysthymia.

On a personal level, the fact that those in the room gained some insight into the "real me" didn't distract from the real purpose of holding the event: I clearly showed that it wasn't easy to talk about mental health, but that didn't need to be an insurmountable barrier to opening up and maybe even asking for help.

What happened next was totally unexpected. One of my colleagues began to talk about her own mental health experiences, something they had never done before in such a public forum. It was an incredibly brave thing to do and I was left feeling both humbled and genuinely moved that someone felt the atmosphere or environment was positive and supportive enough for something so personal to be discussed.

It was a moment of justification and inspiration. This was how good it could be to talk.

CHAPTER 28

TIME TO CONCLUDE

In early 2015, Mind sent me a letter of thanks and a nice certificate of recognition. But the people who deserved to be recognised were those who had been generous enough to make a donation or send messages of encouragement. I thanked every single person who had supported me at the time, and I repeat my sincere thanks now ...

Before I pressed the key to upload the Prozac and Speed blog in 2011, hardly anybody knew I had a mental health condition. The few who did had little idea of how my life had been affected. But through my blogs, subsequent challenges and now this book, I have opened up more than I ever imagined I would ... or could.

In truth, the love and support I have received from those closest to me are the real reasons why I have been able to give a real insight into life with dysthymia. Some of the more reflective and introspective pieces that I've written have hit me very hard from an emotional perspective.

There are memories that were subconsciously suppressed for a reason, and recalling certain times or specific moments in my life brought back feelings that had a significant impact on my mood, and could easily have sent me into one of those horrible downward spirals.

And I suppose 20 … 10 … maybe even five years ago, that is almost certainly what would have happened. But the (hopefully) lasting effect of talking, sharing and challenging myself is that I have a far greater understanding of the ways in which I react to the symptoms of dysthymia. Greater self-awareness doesn't make the feelings go away, but I am so much better at actually saying that something is wrong, rather than waiting to be asked if I'm okay.

I also realise that episodes of dysthymia don't necessarily need a trigger. I would spend hours trying to understand why I felt so low, rather than somehow finding a way firstly to accept the situation and then to fight back. Now I can use my energy to prepare for the fight, because acceptance is no longer such an obstacle.

So, does that mean I'm recovering?

That's a tough question because, although I know I've probably used the word before, I'm not sure that I'll ever be totally free of this chronic condition. Can you class yourself as "recovering" when a full recovery may not be possible?

The word I would prefer to use is "stronger". I'm stronger mentally, I'm stronger physically, and I'm stronger emotionally … well, most of the time!

Yes, I can still occasionally be fragile and vulnerable, but I believe that the most potentially destructive elements of my dysthymia are managed better than at any previous point in my life – and so much of that is down to Elaine.

If you were to ask her, she would say she doesn't make a difference, but that couldn't be further from the truth. She is generous, caring, selfless, dignified and brave. I am blessed to share my life with her.

I suppose that's where my story ends for now.

I've decided to continue raising mental health awareness through talking, sharing experiences and undertaking some brand-new challenges in 2018 and beyond. It's no longer something that I want to do – it's something I *need* to do.

For now, though, whether you are a member of my family, a friend, or someone I haven't met before (or yet), I just want to say a sincere thank you for taking the time to read my story.

I also want to thank everyone at Trigger Press for having faith in me as a person and a writer.

Today might be just like yesterday, and tomorrow may well be just like today. That's the nature of dysthymia, and it's something I've learnt to accept. Because I'm able to talk, I'm able to ask for help and I'm able to fight.

Today might be just like yesterday ... but *actually*, yesterday wasn't too bad at all ...

CHAPTER 29

THE CHALLENGES

2014

1. Raise £1,000 for Mind Charity
2. Spar with a Professional Boxer
3. Sell a Picture I have Painted
4. Have a Game of 501 Against an International Darts Player
5. Meet a Current or Former *Doctor Who* Companion
6. Bowl at a Test Cricketer
7. Get a New Job
8. Bid at an Auction
9. Lose a Stone in Weight
10. Appear on a Radio Show
11. Obtain a Signed Photo from a Tom Baker *Doctor Who* Co-star
12. Meet a Medallist from London 2012
13. Get Invited Backstage at a Gig
14. Hold a Snake
15. Have an Article Printed in a Newspaper
16. See One of my Books on Sale in a High-street Bookshop
17. Visit a Television Studio

18. Receive a Letter from a Member of the Royal Family
19. Have my Head Shaved
20. Obtain a Signed Football Shirt to Auction for Mind
21. Have a Belated First Go on a Rollercoaster
22. Find Someone with the Same Date of Birth as Me
23. Receive a Tweet from a Spice Girl
24. Attempt the Hottest Curry on the Menu
25. Have a Bird of Prey Fly onto my Hand
26. Visit my First Home
27. Get a Tattoo
28. Complete the Novel I Started in 2004
29. Visit my Halls of Residence Room from 1982–83
30. Run Two Miles at Gateshead International Stadium
31. Do a Stand-up Comedy Routine in Front of an Audience
32. Visit a Mosque
33. Climb Roseberry Topping
34. Do Stephanie from Work's Make-up for Her
35. Track Down a Classmate from my First School
36. Get a Photo with an International Rugby League Player
37. Take Part in the Boxing Day Dip in the North Sea
38. Play Goal Shooter in a Netball Team
39. Go Topless on Social Media
40. Be Pictured Outside the Rovers Return

2015

41. Complete a 12-Hour Solo Darts Marathon
42. Meet a Cast Member from *Mrs Brown's Boys*
43. Attempt a 100km Ride on an Exercise Bike
44. Compile a Blog about my Mental Health Experiences for Time to Change

45. Do a Stand-up Comedy Routine for my Middlesbrough Fans!

46. Interview an International Sportswoman

47. Interview an International Sportsman

48. Meet a Second Former *Doctor Who* Companion

49. Meet an Olympic Gold Medallist

50. Observe Ramadan for a Day and Share Reflections with my Muslim Friends

51. Play Badminton Against an England International

52. Present a Radio Show

53. Receive a Letter from my Local MP

54. Take to the Netball Court for a Second (and Definitely Final) Time

2016

55. Complete Dry January

56. Organise a "Time to Talk" Event

57. Update my Book about *Coronation Street* Barmaids for Free Download

58. Meet Someone who has had a Top 10 Single

59. Arrange a Face-to-Face Interview with an International Athlete

60. Complete a Second 12-Hour Darts Marathon

61. Drink Guinness in Dublin

62. Play an International Athlete at His or Her Chosen Sport

63. Spend an Evening Working in a Soup Kitchen

64. Have a Professional Photoshoot

65. Round off my Comedy Career with a Third and Final Gig

66. Meet a Premier League Footballer

67. Be a Racehorse Owner for a Day

68. Obtain a Signed Photo from a Member of Three Randomly Chosen Bands

69. Remember and Correctly Spell the Names of 196 Capital Cities in 15 Minutes

70. Get a Photograph with a Beauty Queen
71. Go Clay Pigeon Shooting
72. Write a Poem
73. Create a Motivational Picture
74. Recreate a Favourite Teenage Photograph
75. Complete the Equivalent of an English Channel Crossing on a Rowing Machine
76. Ready, Steady, Bake!

2017

77. Draw a Pencil Sketch
78. Record a Song
79. Meet an Old School Friend for the First Time in 30 Years
80. Swim a Mile
81. Learn to Knit
82. Put my Old Aching Body Through a Yoga Session
83. Allow Sarah from Work to Dye my Hair Pink
84. Visit my First School
85. Play Table Tennis Against an England International
86. Take Part in a Local Charity Event
87. Repeat #75 but this Time in Less than Three Hours
88. Appear on Television
89. Be Pictured in Front of a Famous National Landmark
90. Release a CD
91. Meet an Actor who has Appeared in *Coronation Street*
92. Write Another Book about *Doctor Who* (1970s Tom Baker Stories)
93. Meet Someone who has had a Number One Single
94. Race Against an Olympic Swimmer

95. Receive a Letter from an Oscar Winner

96. Meet a Special Dog

97. Lose the Weight I've Put Back on Since #9

98. Row a Marathon

99. Visit a Football Ground in Northern Ireland, Scotland, England and Wales in One Day

100. Get a "100" Tattoo as a Permanent Reminder of the Challenges

ACKNOWLEDGEMENTS

Thanks go to Hannah Abrahaley, Sophie Aldred, Daphne Ashbrook, Jay Aston, Emily Austin, Badminton England, Colin Badgery, Jonny Bairstow, Cheryl Baker, Hannah Bayman, Miki Berenyi, Josh Booth, Boris the Golden Eagle, Brothers-in-Ink, Ann Brightwell MBE, Julian Bunn, Esther Burns, Ste Carne, Christian Cawley, the crew at The Chase, Melanie Chisholm, Chris Cook, Gareth Cooper, Sarah Corden-Lloyd, Gordon Cox, Stephanie Cox, Eorl Crabtree, Mo Crilly, Lucienne Crux, Alex Danson MBE, Stephen Devenport, Alexandra Devine, Dhaular Dhar, Glen Durrant, Lewis Edmunds, Yvonne Ferguson, George Friend, Rachael Gage, Ben Gibson, Jon Glen, Grangetown Netball Club, Steph Graham, Lorraine Gray, Anita Harris, Les Harrison, Donna Haynes, Steven Heslewood, Alice Higginbotham, Louise Hobson, Michelle Holmes, the Ireland Netball squad, Jamal's Indian Restaurant, Vesna Jovanovic, Nick Kay, HRH Edward, Duke of Kent, James Kirton, Josh Leather, Rebecca Lee-Bursnall, Maggie Lennard, Hannah Macleod MBE, Emily Maguire, Zakir Mahmoud, Maxi's Mates Rescue and Rehoming Centre, Elaine McCarthy, Jake McCullough, Victoria McGowan, Connor McIntyre, Neil "Mackie" McLennan, Kyle Martin, Gillian Meston, Midchew Pets, Scott Mitchell, Diane Mondal, Anthony "Morry" Morrison, Joanne Moss, Malcolm Muldoon, Nìamh Murphy, Imran Naeem, Keith Nicholson, Mike Nolan, One Ummah, Judith Paris, Mike Parr, Helen Parsons, Mike Peters, Katrina Power, Andrew Powles, Alan Ransome OBE, Danny Reed, Vicky Rees, Kate Richardson-Walsh OBE, Rico the Lurcher, Paul Sinha, Stephanie Rowe, Steve and Bernice Roe, Georgina Sayers, Allyson Smith, The Stand Comedy Club, Sarah Stringer, Dawn Suffell, Emma Thompson, Heidi Thompson, Chris Thorman, Sarah Treanor, Hannah Trimble, Lee Tuck, Anna Turley MP, Jeff Turner, Runa Uddin, Vicky Urquhart, John Waite, Rhys Walker, Jenny Wallwork, Bradley Walsh, Justin Welch, Nicola White MBE, Geraldine Williams, Gary Wilson, Amanda Woods, Jen Wytcherley, John Young.

the *Shaw* mind
FOUNDATION

Creating hope for children,
adults and families

Sign up to our charity, The Shaw Mind Foundation
www.shawmindfoundation.org
and keep in touch with us; we would love to hear from you.

*We aim to bring to an end the suffering and despair caused
by mental health issues. Our goal is to make help and support
available for every single person in society, from all walks of life.
We will never stop offering hope. These are our promises.*

TRIGGERPRESS
The voice of mental health

www.trigger-press.com

Trigger Press is a publishing house devoted to opening conversations about mental health. We tell the stories of people who have suffered from mental illnesses and recovered, so that others may learn from them.

Adam Shaw is a worldwide mental health advocate and philanthropist. Now in recovery from mental health issues, he is committed to helping others suffering from debilitating mental health issues through the global charity he co-founded, The Shaw Mind Foundation. www.shawmindfoundation.org

Lauren Callaghan (CPsychol, PGDipClinPsych, PgCert, MA (hons), LLB (hons), BA), born and educated in New Zealand, is an innovative industry-leading psychologist based in London, United Kingdom. Lauren has worked with children and young people, and their families, in a number of clinical settings providing evidence based treatments for a range of illnesses, including anxiety and obsessional problems. She was a psychologist at the specialist national treatment centres for severe obsessional problems in the UK and is renowned as an expert in the field of mental health, recognised for diagnosing and successfully treating OCD and anxiety related illnesses in particular. In addition to appearing as a treating clinician in the critically acclaimed and BAFTA award-winning documentary *Bedlam*, Lauren is a frequent guest speaker on mental health conditions in the media and at academic conferences. Lauren also acts as a guest lecturer and honorary researcher at the Institute of Psychiatry Kings College, UCL.

Please visit the link below:

www.trigger-press.com

Join us and follow us...

@trigger_press
@Shaw_Mind

Search **The Shaw Mind Foundation** on Facebook
Search **Trigger Press** on Facebook